D1633261

PROFESSOR JAMES MITCHELL holds the chair in
of the Academy of Government at the University
held chairs at the University of Strathclyde and Sheffield. His research has included studies of political parties and public opinion in Scotland. His most recent work has included studies of the SNP, Scottish elections and the independence referendum. All of his work is informed by an appreciation of the importance of the past in its impact on current concerns.

Hamilton 1967

The By-Election That Transformed Scotland

JAMES MITCHELL

Luath Press Limited
EDINBURGH
www.luath.co.uk

First published 2017

ISBN: 978-1-912147-22-9

The paper used in this book is recyclable. It is made from
low chlorine pulps produced in a low energy, low emissions manner
from renewable forests.

Printed and bound by
Ashford Colour Press, Gosport

Typeset in 11.5 point Sabon
by 3btype.com

The authors' right to be identified as author of this work under the
Copyright, Designs and Patents Act 1988 has been asserted.

© James Mitchell 2017

Contents

Timeline

1966

31 March	General Election. Labour wins an overall majority of 97 with 46 seats of Scotland's 71 seats and 49.8% of the vote. SNP win 5% of the vote standing in 23 seats, saving 13 deposits.[1]
25 May	Government announces membership of Royal Commission on Local Government in Scotland under chair of Lord Wheatley.
16 May	National Union of Seamen go on strike
23 May	Government declares a State of Emergency as seamen's strike affects international trade.
15 June	David Steel MP's Abortion Bill gets second reading in Commons.
29 June	Premier Harold Wilson distances himself from US bombings in Vietnam.
1 July	Bank rate raised to 7% and special deposits doubled.
3 July	Frank Cousins resigns as Minister for Technology in opposition to Government's prices and incomes policy.
4 July	Prices and Incomes Board legislation published.
5 July	Leo Abse introduces Sexual Offences Bill legalising homosexuality but Bill does not extend to Scotland.
14 July	Gwynfor Evans wins Carmarthen by-election and becomes the first ever Plaid Cymru MP.
20 July	Wage freeze and package of £500m cuts to avoid speculation against sterling.
29 July	White Paper proposes compulsory wages freeze.

30 July	England wins World Cup.
4 August	25 Labour MPs abstain in vote on Prices and Incomes Bill.
19 October	Russell Johnston, Liberal MP, introduces Scottish Self-Government Bill.
10 November	Wilson Government formally announces it will seek membership of EEC.
16–17 November	Commons debates membership of EEC – both main parties divided on issue.
1967	
18 January	Jeremy Thorpe becomes leader of the Liberal Party.
7 February	National Front founded.
2 March	Harold Wilson warns Labour backbenchers against rebelling, 'every dog is allowed one bite, but a different view is taken of a dog that goes on biting'.
22 March	Iron and Steel Act passed – nationalising an important Lanarkshire industry.
9 March	Glasgow Pollok by-election – Conservatives take seat from Labour and SNP wins 28.2%. Plaid Cymru win 39.9% but defeated by Labour with 49.0% in Rhondda West by-election.
21 April	Queen's Speech. Government announces intention to join EEC if safeguards for Commonwealth agreed
2 May	Formal announcement that UK would apply for EEC membership
	Local elections. SNP win 60,000 votes (23 per cent) in Glasgow but no seats on the council.
3 May	Budget imposes Selective Employment Tax in effort to shift employment from service sector

	to declining manufacturing sector, on which Lanarkshire is heavily dependent.
10 May	Vote on EEC membership in carried 34 Labour MPs vote against and 51 abstain; 26 Conservatives and one Liberal voted against.
16 May	De Gaulle states at press conference that UK was not ready for EEC membership.
18–20 May	Scottish Liberal Party conference rejects call from Ludovic Kennedy for a pact with the SNP.
2–4 June	SNP annual conference
20 July	Justice Latey Committee recommends reducing age of majority from 21 to 18.
24 July	Chancellor of Exchequer Jim Callaghan dismisses devaluation as a policy for Government.
25 July	Government enacts an increase in family allowance to come into effect from October but provokes resignation of Peggy Herbison, veteran Labour Minister and Lanarkshire MP who viewed it as too little.
28 August	Cabinet re-shuffle with Harold Wilson taking overall responsibility for the economy.
18 September	Start of dock strikes in London and Liverpool.
21 September	Conservatives gain Cambridge and Walthamstow West from Labour in by-elections.
8 October	Clement Attlee dies.
27 October	Abortion Act passed.
31 October	Queen's Speech includes commitment to abolish hereditary peers.
2 November	HAMILTON BY-ELECTION. WINNIE EWING WINS SEAT FOR SNP FROM LABOUR.

18 November	Devaluation of £ sterling.
23 November	West Derbyside by-election – Labour falls to third place behind Liberals.
24 November	Launch of 'Thistle Group' inside the Conservative Party arguing for home rule.
November	Devaluation of £ sterling.

1968

16 January	Cuts in public spending announced.
19 March	Budget introduces deflationary package of measures.
11 April	STUC conference comes out in favour of devolution.
9 May	SNP wins 30% of vote and 108 seats in local government elections, with 37.2% of vote in Glasgow and 13 councillors elected including George Leslie.
18 May	Ted Heath makes his 'Declaration of Perth' at Scottish Conservative Party conference and announces the establishment of committee under Sir Alec Douglas-Home.
18–21 September	Liberal Party Assembly opposes a call for Scottish independence in favour of a federal scheme.
	Passenger road transport and sea transport transferred to Scottish Office.

1969

15 April	Harold Wilson appoints a Royal Commission under Labour Crowther to consider the Constitution.
6 May	Local elections. SNP makes only modest gains which are interpreted as a setback.

25 September	Publication of Report of the Royal Commission on the Scottish Local Government under Lord Wheatley.
30 October	Glasgow Gorbals by-election. Labour wins seat with 53.4% with SNP in second place with 25.0% – interpreted as setback for SNP.
1970	
19 March	Report of Scottish Constitutional Committee – under Sir Alec Douglas-Home and appointed by Ted Heath – issued, recommending an elected Scottish Convention.
19 March	South Ayrshire by-election. Jim Sillars holds the seat comfortably for Labour with 54.1% and SNP win 20.4% of vote.
18 June	General Election. SNP contests 65 constituencies and wins 11.4% of vote. Hamilton is lost but Western Isles is gained from Labour. Conservatives returned to power.
October	The giant Forties oil field discovered by BP in the central North Sea.
1979	
1 March	1st Scottish Devolution Referendum. 51.6% vote for creation of Scottish Assembly but insufficient turnout to reach the required 40% of electorate voting Yes.
1997	
11 September	2nd Scottish Devolution Referendum. Scotland votes overwhelmingly Yes Yes to create Scottish Parliament and devolve some tax raising powers.
1999	
12 May	Scottish Parliament opens with Winnie Ewing MSP stating 'I want to start with the words that I have always wanted either to say or to hear

	someone else say – the Scottish Parliament, which adjourned on 25 March 1707, is hereby reconvened.'
2007	
16 May	Alex Salmond becomes Scotland's first SNP First Minister, leading a minority government following the Holyrood election on 3 May.
2011	
5 May	SNP win unexpected overall majority in Holyrood election.
2014	
18 September	1st Scottish Independence Referendum. Scotland votes 55% No, 45% Yes.
20 November	Nicola Sturgeon becomes 2nd SNP First Minister of Scotland.
2015	
7 May	SNP win 56 out of 59 Westminster seats in UK general election.
2016	
5 May	SNP lose overall majority in Holyrood election and form administation with support of Scottish Green Party.
2017	
8 June	SNP reduced from 56 to 35 Westminster seats in Theresa May's snap general election.

Preface

THE IMMEDIATE IDEA for this book was the forthcoming 50th anniversary of the Hamilton by-election held on 2 November 1967. Having worked on the subject over many years, conducted numerous interviews, surveyed SNP members, delved in the archives and trawled through newspapers and other contemporary sources, the anniversary offered an opportunity to reflect on the crucial turning point in Scottish politics in the 1960s. In writing *The Scottish Question* (Oxford University Press 2014), I became aware that, despite the wealth of material on the subject, we still had not come close to understanding Scotland's transition from a stable two-party system to the multi-party system that now exists and that the role and nature of Scottish nationalism, particularly how it has evolved as an ideology, required more attention focused on this period.

Much has been written in an attempt to explain the rise of the SNP and the wider political and social developments at that time. It proved fruitful to read these accounts again. Many have not aged well but a remarkable number remain fresh and valuable. It was particularly pleasing to read work by my late colleague Jack Brand. In the 1960s, Jack was Director of the Survey Research Centre at Strathclyde University and contributed hugely to our understanding of Scottish politics. It was a privilege to co-direct the 1992 Scottish Election Study with him, drawing on his long experience and deep understanding of political behaviour. His impish demeanour challenged and charmed in equal measure but his depth of knowledge of Scottish politics and history, national movements in Europe and political science were enviable.

Much of Jack's work used here was in the form of journalism submitted to various newspapers. These newspapers were invaluable in understanding developments in Hamilton. The local *Hamilton Advertiser* was a key source for this book. Not only did it bring the by-election to life, but reading through more than two years of the paper helped me understand the everyday life in the constituency. The Scottish Boundary Commission helped supply information on Hamilton's 1967 boundaries and I gratefully acknowledge Crown Copyright, Ordnance Survey for allowing me to use the map of the constituency at the start of Chapter Two.

I was keen to speak to some of those involved in the 1967 campaign and it was both enlightening and fun to meet and discuss matters with a number of locals who had been involved. Tom Muir, Helen Moir, James Price, Ian and Margaret Gourlay, Les Cordingley, Jack Foley, Barbara Samson and Alan Forsyth had great tales to tell and recollections of the campaign. John McAteer, Winnie Ewing's election agent, was by all accounts an important figure who sadly died in 1977, but his widow, Kate, offered fascinating insights into the campaign and the very human nature of political activism. Kate's home was the headquarters of the campaign until a shop at Peacock Cross was acquired and she supplied tea and digestives after an evening's canvassing. This side of political campaigning is all too often overlooked by cynics who view political activists as a species apart from normal people. As much as anything this book is a celebration of political activism (of all political persuasions).

Fergus and Annabelle Ewing answered many questions and recounted stories from their childhood or pointed me in the direction of those who might. They also kindly arranged for me to visit and interview their mother. Fergus provided me with two photographs from the campaign. I am very grateful to the Scottish Political Archive at Stirling University for kind permission to use other photographs in the book. I had interviewed Winnie Ewing at various times over many years but this book was an opportunity to focus on the by-election. Whenever she was pressed on some aspect of her role, she would shift the conversation to emphasise the role played by others, particularly Robert McIntyre, John McAteer, Hugh MacDonald and, of course, the enormous support she was given by her late husband Stewart. It is difficult to measure the importance of those who contribute in the background to lively political debate. For every successful – and indeed unsuccessful – candidate, there are usually scores of other politicians who do not seek the limelight. The notion that they are all out for themselves is a view that could only be held by those utterly ignorant of the workings of democratic politics.

Academic colleagues were also helpful with advice and comments. Paula Somerville was very helpful. Paula's *Through the Maelstrom* (Stirling 2013) is an excellent detailed account covering the period discussed. David Rollo, son of the SNP's Hamilton candidate in 1959, was generous in supplying information and ideas. My PhD student Thomas Stewart offered a fine critical reading through draft chapters. Particular thanks must go to Ewen Cameron of Strathclyde University who read through chapters offering remarkably helpful detailed comments. Ewen brought sources to my attention that I would have missed. I want to thank Cliff Williamson, historian of Bath Spa University, for his encylopaedic knowledge of politics and society in the period covered, but mostly for lending support and helping me get this finished. My son Euan helped with research for the book. He spent considerable time diligently researching *Hansard* online – and found himself in a world that was well before he was born. He became fascinated in Biafra and the Nigerian Civil War, which Winnie Ewing engaged with at length during her time as Hamilton's MP. Euan was born two months after the Scottish Parliament came into being and now has a better understanding than most of his generation of the period that marked the transition between two very different periods in Scottish politics.

Much of the research was conducted in the National Library of Scotland, including the archives. Other sources used in the book are drawn from the National Archives at Kew, west London and the Bodleain Library in Oxford. The University of Edinburgh Library, including its Centre for Research Collections, provided many sources. Gavin MacDougall at Luath was typically supportive of this project.

Luath provides a great service to authors and the public that we ought to celebrate. Gavin MacDougall and Luath continue to be a major asset to public life in Scotland. Books on Scottish politics were few and far between before 1967. Luath has ensured that many works that might otherwise never have found a publisher are available and contribute to debate and understanding as will, no doubt, be important sources for future historians.

In my research, I came across reference to a young couple who had been married the day before the by-election and then spent the day in rainy Hamilton campaigning for Winnie Ewing. I tried to track them down and had all but given up when I received an email from Grant Thoms, editor of the *Scots Independent*. Unknown to me, my initial enquiry had been passed on through a number of people – Ian McCann, Ian Hudghton, Ian Hamilton and Irene McGugan. Irene sent me contact details for Tom and Ruth Walker with whom I corresponded. The book's Introduction provides an account of the night of the count drawn from what they wrote for their SNP branch newsletter.

Finally, I recall Jack Brand taking issue with someone who offered a cheap, cynical shot at political activists at an academic conference many years ago. In his erudite, polite way Jack reminded us all that political activists were not, as the cynic had suggested, 'swivel eyed' extremists but the backbone to any democracy. This book is dedicated to Jack's memory and to the unsung heroes of democracy in all democratic political parties.

Introduction

From the start of Harold Wilson's second term of office the government started to lose by-election seats in rapid succession. The years of this administration proved a watershed in British by-election history: out of 37 contests the government was defeated in almost half.[1]

[Hamilton] had a tremendous impact on Scottish public opinion... This election really marked the arrival of the SNP for the majority of the Scottish electorate as a party with a serious political future.[2]

Victory in the rain

TWO CAR LOADS of SNP supporters left Arbroath in the early hours of the morning of the Hamilton by-election in November 1967. One car included a couple who had married the day before, on the bride's birthday. Tam and Ruth Walker, along with Jim McGugan who would be SNP candidate in many elections over subsequent years, were founder members of the Arbroath branch of the SNP. The honeymoon couple spent polling day handing out last minute leaflets in the rain in High Blantyre. The unexpected weather meant that a Mary Quant-style plastic raincoat had to be bought for Ruth. A photograph of the couple appeared in the next day's *Daily Record*.[3] They represented an important part of the explanation for the election of Winnie Ewing as SNP MP for what had been one of Labour's safest seats in Parliament. There was an enthusiasm and energy in the SNP ranks that was absent amongst the main parties.

The couple offered their 'eye-witness' account of events outside the count at St John's School in Hamilton in their branch newsletter. It captures the excitement and idealism of these young SNP supporters. They thought that every car in the car park appeared to be covered with 'Vote Ewing' posters and reported that SNP leader Arthur

Donaldson thought the SNP had a 'strong chance'. Pipes and guitars were being played despite heavy rain and SNP activists were singing the 1960s protest song, 'We shall overcome'. The crowd kept calling on Winnie Ewing to come out as they awaited the declaration. The count was over about 15 minutes after midnight and journalists rushed to phones to call news desks but the crowd outside could still only speculate. Even when the returning officer appeared with a smiling Ewing, the Arbroath members reported, 'We know we have won yet we do not know'. The Tory candidate followed and spoke to Ewing while Labour's Alex Wilson stood back, understandably deflated.

When the result was declared, though the precise figure was muffled by the crowd, the emotional energy of a small fringe party that had not seen victory since a by-election in the very unusual circumstances of the closing stages of the Second World War, was released, 'Dancing, singing, shouting, drunker than any alcohol could ever make us. Drunk with joy and victory. One young woman is helped away in tears streaming down her cheeks. Another Nationalist wanders about dreamily, carrying half a banner staff.' But these foot soldiers, who remain the SNP's main strength, were aware that this victory was only the start. As quoted from an article by Magnus Magnusson that had appeared in *The Scotsman* earlier in the week supporting Ewing, 'Now let the real battle commence'.[4]

Few are aware that the campaign started well over a year before polling day. The issues raised are largely forgotten and the extent to which victory was cause or effect in the growing support for the SNP has never been disentangled. There have been competing interpretations of the SNP success with some emphasising macro-level developments including the decline of Empire and Britain's place in the world, signifying a weakening of British nationalism; major socio-economic changes disrupting traditional patterns of political behaviour; the context of the swinging Sixties when new political and social movements arose; the unpopularity of a Labour Government that had over-promised at the previous year's general election and struggled to cope with major challenges; the greatly improved organisational capacity of the SNP. Other explanations focus on the party, its activists and, of course, the candidate herself. We do not have opinion poll data from Hamilton, or even for Scotland, that can assist the study of the event. Local election results gave little hint of the SNP victory. The evidence in assessing the causes of the SNP breakthrough is necessarily speculative and it therefore must be treated with care. Assertions have been made and become accepted wisdom that need to be questioned. Some claims prove to be inaccurate or at least exaggerated on inspection.

Hamilton 1967 raises many 'What ifs...?' What if John Smith, later leader of the Labour Party, had won the Labour nomination having it made to the short list? What if there had been a snap by-election, rather than more than a year-long campaign? What if Harold Wilson's cabinet of impressive intellects but massive egos had managed to cohere better and given a better appearance of competence in difficult circumstances? What if the Liberals had stood a candidate? None of these questions can be answered with full confidence but each is another way of asking why the SNP won.

This book is based on the evidence that could be provided, including interviews with some of the key figures involved and relies on archives of the SNP papers and of leading figures such as Arthur Donaldson and Dr Robert McIntyre. There is also heavy reliance on newspaper reports, including the local *Hamilton Advertiser*, and the main daily and Sunday newspapers. Media coverage of the by-election was understandably limited until late in the campaign though there is much of value to be found in the local paper in the two years prior to the by-election that helps us understand the context, issues and nature of Hamilton politics and society. It is tempting to focus simply on the decline of the coal industry and view the area as a place on the verge of post-industrialisation but Hamilton was buzzing with activity in the mid to late 1960s. There is as much, indeed probably more, evidence of reasons to be optimistic than pessimistic than might be imagined. Viewed from when events unfolded leading up to the by-election, many people in Hamilton were excited and hopeful about the future. The SNP message was as mixed as was the mood of the times – critical of government failure but offering a positive alternative.

Many of the issues then being discussed remain with us today. Harold Wilson's Government had applied for membership of the European Economic Community and the UK's relations with Europe was a recurring theme at the time. Scotland's constitutional status and whether Scotland should have its own voice in negotiations has resonated down the years. The role of women in Scottish politics was discussed. The issue of young voters and the age of majority would arise in the by-election and afterwards. As today, the mid-late 1960s were a period of political and economic turbulence. Old certainties were being questioned and old loyalties strained. These phenomena were not restricted to Scotland. Hamilton was, in this sense, emblematic of the age.

By-elections

By-elections come and go, attracting immediate attention, much speculation and exaggerated interpretations of their impact. New dawns beckon and minor parties assume, or at least hope, that a by-election success signals a breakthrough. In 1962, the Liberals' much awaited revival was thought to have been signalled by victory at Orpington. That came to little; though the Liberals did go on to win more seats, including David Steel's victory at the Roxburgh, Selkirk and Peebles by-election in 1965. In the 1980s, the Social Democrats scored a number of by-election victories suggesting that a major realignment was underway in British politics. In the event, it fizzled out. By-elections are not good guides as to what is likely to happen at any subsequent general election. Spectacular by-election gains more often than not return to the party that had lost the seat and by-election victories rarely tell us much about underlying political developments.

But equally, by-elections are more than just local concerns. They can be important media events not only because they may be the only electoral show in town and may highlight, in exaggerated form, some underlying trends. Carefully considered, along with longer term trends and other evidence, by-elections are tests – tests that need to be repeated to be sure that they are not occasional political spasms. Before devolution, by-elections had a significance in Scottish politics. They were uniquely Scottish political events. General elections were British political contests with the Scottish dimension overwhelmed by the debate on who should be Prime Minister. Scottish local elections rarely attracted the same attention but a by-election was Scottish theatre, rarely performed but often with an interesting cast. The establishment of the Scottish Parliament removed this distinction and by-elections are now less significant than they were pre-devolution.

The evolution of interpretations of the Hamilton by-election has been cyclical. In its immediate aftermath, it was widely thought to signify major change in Scottish politics but within three years Hamilton was dismissed as a protest vote. Within another four years, Hamilton 1967 again assumed significance as the harbinger of major change but by 1979 was once more being dismissed. Today, it is seen as significant but whether as cause or consequence of longer term change is not always clear. There have been ebbs and flows but the SNP has had a continuous presence in the House of Commons since Hamilton.

Even if a by-election tells us less about underlying trends than might be immediately imagined, such interpretations can themselves create change. Hamilton 1967 was thought to be significant by the Labour Government and Conservative Opposition at Westminster and thereby caused change. There had been periodic spasms of support for home rule with Government reactions developing Scotland's position in the union, but the reaction to Hamilton set Scotland on a long, though far from certain, route to the establishment of the Scottish Parliament. Labour and Conservative Parties set up enquiries, dabbled with constitutional change and emphasised their Scottish credentials. Whitehall woke up to the Scottish Question in 1967 as never before. The idea that there was a Scottish political system[5] caused an increase in the amount of media attention paid to Scottish politics.

CHAPTER ONE

Turbulent politics, economic security and insecurity

> In all our plans for the future, we are re-defining and we are re-stating our Socialism in terms of the scientific revolution. But that revolution cannot become a reality unless we are prepared to make far-reaching changes in economic and social attitudes which permeate our whole system of society. The Britain that is going to be forged in the white heat of this revolution will be no place for restrictive practices or for outdated methods on either side of industry.[1]

> Modernisation is a homogenizing process... Modernisation produces tendencies toward convergence among societies. Modernisation involves movement 'toward an interdependence among politically organised societies and toward an ultimate integration of societies.' The 'universal imperatives of modern ideas and institutions' may lead to a stage 'at which the various societies are so homogeneous as to be capable of forming a world state'.[2]

Introduction

IN THE EARLY 1960s, the United Kingdom was thought to be a stable democracy, growing in prosperity and optimism. Labour's leader Harold Wilson caught the mood with his 1963 party conference speech tapping into this sense of modernisation, progress and increased opportunities. The occasional by-election upset did little to dent the sense that Britain's two party system remained intact. Britain looked politically united. This was the period when British politics was assumed to be dominated by class. Peter Pulzer's famous claim, published in the year of the Hamilton by-election, that class was the 'basis of British politics; all else is embellishment and detail'[3] was the dominant view at this time.

Perennial Scottish Question

The 'Scottish Question' has never been answered definitively. Nor can it be. The notion that there ever was a 'settled will' speaks more of hope than reality. The relationship between Scotland and London/ rest of the UK (rUK) has occasionally risen up the political agenda. There have been periods of relative calm but these have invariably been disrupted by periods of grievance and demands for reform of one kind and another. But these were disruptions rather than ruptures. Every generation needs to address these matters. What is striking is the extent to which successive UK governments responded, perhaps half-heartedly, with reforms in the relationship. The main reason why the Scottish Question can never be answered definitively is that the context keeps changing and therefore the Question requires a new response to meet new demands. Arrangements created in 1707 were of limited relevance to future generations. The autonomous Kirk played a more significant part in the life of Scottish society than it would for later generations. The era of the night watchman state required different institutions from those of the emerging welfare state. Periods of rapid change appear to bring with them concerns that the relationships involved in the Scottish Question are no longer working adequately.

Discontent has rarely focused on clear alternative arrangements. In the mid to late 19th century, focus was on gaining a Government Minister with a seat in the Cabinet to look after Scottish interests at the heart of government but even that was vague, as supporters gave little thought as to the precise responsibilities of the Scottish Minister. Demands for home rule would be made over subsequent decades throughout the 20th century but these were vague on detail. Just as the demand changed, so too did those making the demand. The demand for a Scottish Minister in the latter half of the 19th century was made by a wide range of interests including the press and Scotland's then two main parties (Liberals and Conservatives). Demand for home rule in the 20th century came from Labour and the Liberals as well as an assortment of pressure groups.

The Scottish National Party is today associated with the demand for independence but, for most of its pre-Hamilton history, was but one of a number of organisations arguing for home rule. It became the main vehicle for Scots to express disenchantment with the way Scotland was governed in the latter half of the 20th century, arguably from the Hamilton by-election. The SNP was founded through a merger of two tiny parties in 1934 and operated of the fringe of Scottish politics advocating 'self-government', a term that allowed for a variety of interpretations. *Independence* was not a major part of its lexicon during its first three decades and it would have been difficult for most Scots to distinguish between what the SNP advocated from proposals coming from radical Labour MPs in the inter-war period or Scottish Liberals who supported *home rule*. The SNP considered various options over the years but never needed to offer a clear prospectus as it was never a serious threat to its opponents, until Hamilton.

Successive UK Governments responded to these grievances with a variety of reforms; giving Scotland a voice at the centre in government, parliamentary reforms to take account of Scottish distinctiveness, and more public policy resources but they fell well short of giving Scotland any kind of self-government. There would be efforts to present these concessions as forms of self-government which may simply have legitimised the demand for autonomy. It would have been unwise of any UK government to imagine that it had solved the Scottish Question and there have been unwise, but rarely insensitive, UK Governments. Often enough, Scottish grievances would coincide with, and no doubt were partly caused by, wider challenges facing governments. The rise of the SNP made demands more concrete than previously and more threatening to the main parties that formed governments in London. The demand was emphatically for a Parliament, even if its precise status was unclear.

Demand for a Scottish Parliament after the Second World War attracted considerable attention. Supporters claimed that around two million Scots had signed the 'Scottish Covenant', essentially a petition, in favour of home rule. An implausible aim of gathering three million signatures was made by one of the leading campaigners.[4] The SNP was not central to this campaign. Reforms in Parliamentary procedure followed, introduced by the Labour Government, and the Conservatives promised a Royal Commission on Scottish Affairs which was established when they came back to office and reported in 1954. Its report concluded that, 'History shows that misunderstandings due to thoughtlessness, lack of tact and disregard of sentiment can be serious' and warned against, 'needless English thoughtlessness and undue Scottish susceptibilities'. It noted the changed context lying behind Scottish grievances.[5] Minor administrative reforms followed as demand for reform passed.

At the time of the Covenant, it seemed that buying time with a Royal Commission worked in kicking the issue into the long grass. By the time the Royal Commission report was published, the sense of grievance had diminished. The SNP performed poorly at the 1955 election and, by the late 1950s, many assumed that all was well. Scottish nationalism's obituary was written in two articles in the *Glasgow Herald* in 1959 by R.D. Kernohan, a Tory supporting journalist. Kernohan argued that the union had been shaken for ten months in 1949–50 and that his party had 'appeased' the Scots with proposals for 'administrative devolution and the restoration of a free economy'. Labour had been committed to home rule from when Keir Hardie stood as the first independent Labour candidate in the mid-Lanarkshire by-election in 1888. But this commitment had competed with a belief that equality required a strong central government and support for uniformity of policies across the state.

By the late 1950s, Labour had abandoned its support for Scottish home rule. By 1959, only the Liberals supported home rule and the SNP supported some 'freely negotiated agreement' but neither came close to a breakthrough though Kernohan accepted that 'even a substantial minority of seats would put the present form of union in serious danger'.[6] Three years later, former SNP leader James Halliday maintained that between 6 and 12 SNP seats would be enough to force change.[7]

A key theme of elections in Scotland over the 20th century was for the main opposition party to accuse the governing party of neglecting Scotland, contributing to the inability to *solve* the Scottish Question. While Labour and the Conservatives avoided promising home rule, each fuelled the sense of grievance in attacks on the other and kept the Scottish Question alive. An editorial in the *Hamilton Advertiser* in May 1967 captured this well: 'When Labour came to national power in the autumn of 1964, lavish promises were made. Scotland, it was said, had been overlooked by the Tories; a Labour Scotland would attend to Scotland's interests, bringing new industries, reversing the emigration trends, and revitalising the whole life of the nation. These promises have conspicuously failed. A few incidents, such as the NALGO pay-rise refusal, have been seen as pointers to a London-orientated government which has Scotland at the periphery of their interest. The Scottish Nationalists have made ground in a situation that might have been specially made for them.'[8]

Economic turbulence

The front page of *Hamilton Advertiser*'s first issue of 1967 carried news that 'Ironmonger's son becomes Sir Alex [sic]',[9] a reference to the knighthood awarded to Alec Cairncross in the New Year's honours list. Sir Alec was born in Lesmahagow, about 14 miles south east of Hamilton and had attended Hamilton Academy before embarking on a career that led to becoming head of the Government Economic

Service (GES). Cairncross's diary recorded key meetings and economic issues facing the country at the start of what would prove to be a politically and economically turbulent year. Incomes policy, membership of the European Economic Community, bank rates, devaluation, budget deficits were all high on the government's agenda. At the end of January, he met Bobby Kennedy – 'very young, handsome, almost undergraduate' – at a Ditchley conference on the Common Market and North Atlantic Free Trade Area (NAFTA).[10] In 1967, Harold Wilson's Government would be rebuffed in its efforts to join the Common Market by French President De Gaulle. At Ditchley, Kennedy noted the rising influence of nationalism but the nationalism he had in mind was in Asia and Africa.[11] Scottish nationalism did not register on the political radar of the elites who assembled at Ditchley at the start of 1967. These international economic developments would not only occupy the head of the GES but would have an impact on the Lanarkshire economy. Lanarkshire depended on international trade as much as any part of Britain. Coal production had declined sharply. Colville's steel works was the biggest employer in Hamilton though sitting outside the constituency.

The Scottish economy lagged behind the rest of Britain for a long time and various efforts had been made by successive London Governments to tackle this relative weakness. One notable feature of these efforts was the growing acceptance of the existence of a distinct Scottish economy. An enquiry into the state of the Scottish economy that was published in 1961[12] led to the Central Scotland Plan, issued by the Government. It sought to 'modernise' the Scottish economy. *Modernisation* was a loose and much used term in the 1960s, as it would be in its many reincarnations afterwards. Crucially, there was a cross-party consensus that the state could and should intervene. There were differences between the two main parties but considerable agreement in broad terms. The emphasis was on planning with new planning institutions and instruments set up in the 1960s. The Scottish Development Department was created within the Scottish Office in 1963 and the Highlands and Islands Development Board in 1965. Regional policy was intended to even out opportunities across the state. The Industrial Development Act, 1966 created new development areas which included almost all of Scotland. The following year 'Special Development Areas' – small areas hit hard by pit closures – were created with three in Scotland, including Lanarkshire.[13] There were concerns with Scotland's relative economic condition but also optimism that planning would address these concerns.

But economic crises afflicting the UK as a whole undermined efforts. In July 1966, the Labour Government, just over three months after winning a landslide majority, was imposing massive cuts in expenditure, more severe than those that had undermined Attlee's Labour Government in 1949. A wages freeze was imposed that lasted through to early 1967. There was mounting pressure to devalue the pound sterling with ongoing debates in the Cabinet, spilling over into the public, contributing to the sense that all was not well.

It would be wrong to conclude that all was doom and gloom in the lead up to the by-election. There were significant good news stories. It is conceivable that these played into the SNP's appeal more than the stories of doom and gloom. In late September 1967, Scottish school children were marshalled into school halls to peer at television screens to watch the Queen arrive at John Brown's shipyard on Clydeside to launch the QE2, the last great transatlantic ocean liners. Aside from the economy, there were other reasons for buoyancy and optimism. In May 1967, at least a section of Hamilton's population celebrated Celtic's victory in the European cup final, the first British team (and indeed Northern European – with the previous winners being from Italy, Spain and Portugal) to win the European Cup. The 'Lisbon Lions' were almost all local to Celtic Park. Home grown success on the football field did not translate directly into politics but might well have contributed to the sense that anything was possible. Hamilton was lively culturally, including a vibrant local jazz scene. This mix of challenges, optimism, worries and sense of change played into the backdrop with disruptive effects on attitudes and values.

Europe and the world

It is difficult to know the extent to which the UK's standing in the world and collective self-perception affected political behaviour. Scotland had been at the heart of Empire and many Scots had been beneficiaries. The end of Empire and withdrawal from East of Suez were agonizing decisions for the UK's elites keen to maintain a global role and reputation. Alternative paths were sought. While there is little direct evidence that the rise of the SNP was linked to the decline of Empire, the most rigorous analysis of this relationship in the 1960s demonstrates that the international context created a 'favourable climate' for the SNP.[14] In 1963, the country had, in the words of former American Secretary of State Dean Acheson, 'lost an Empire and has not yet found a role'. In 1957, the leaders of six European governments signed the Treaty of Rome to establish the European Economic Community. The United Kingdom did not join West Germany, France, Italy, Belgium, Netherlands and Luxembourg. Having initially stood aloof, the UK soon changed its mind. In July 1961, Prime Minister Harold Macmillan argued that membership of the EEC was a 'political as well as an economic issue' and that the UK would formally apply for negotiations to join.[15] A variety of reasons lay behind this change of heart: a perception that the EEC had been successful in helping post-war European economic recovery, contrary to early expectations; the relative failure of the European Free Trade Association, which had been Britain's alternative to EEC membership; declining trade with the Commonwealth; and strong encouragement from the United States. Hugh Gaitskell, Labour's then leader, was highly sceptical and would warn that EEC membership risked becoming a federation which would 'mean the end of

Britain as an independent European state. It means the end of a thousand years of history.'[16] President De Gaulle of France vetoed the application to the annoyance of other member states.

Harold Wilson had a different view from his Labour predecessor and instigated another application for membership after becoming Prime Minister. Wilson won Labour Party endorsement for the application at his party's annual conference at Scarborough in October 1967 but a significant minority opposed membership. Both main British parties were internally divided on Europe. An estimate in May 1967 suggested that six of the 21 Cabinet members were opposed, plus four others unless important concessions were granted.[17] Amongst those firmly in the opposition camp was Scottish Secretary Willie Ross. But Labour's application met the same Gaullist veto as had the Conservatives'. In late October 1967, Wilson was reportedly threatening to pull out of various European commitments – withdrawing the 50,000 strong British army on the Rhine; boycotting the four powers agreement on Berlin; abandoning support for German reunification; and reducing Britain's role in Western European defence – if its EEC membership application was rejected.[18] It was an odd sort of diplomacy but one that would run through UK relations with the EEC (and European Union) from before it joined up to its decision to leave and beyond.

The SNP was as divided as the two main British parties. Few noticed what the SNP was thinking about European integration when it was on the fringe of Scottish politics. It had passed a resolution in favour of European unity in 1948 and a leading member had attended the Hague Congress which led to the creation of the European Movement, at which Winston Churchill had famously referred to the need to create a 'kind of United States of Europe'.[19] Through the 1950s, articles and opinions suggested that the SNP favoured membership of the EEC. But there was always scepticism in the ranks and this grew in the 1960s as the party expanded and brought in people who were suspicious of the EEC, seeing it as a centralising, bureaucratic institution of the Cold War. Billy Wolfe, who became a prominent figure and party leader in 1969, was highly sceptical. The SNP articulated a position that united most views in the party. It argued for membership but on Scottish terms, allowing opponents of membership to blame London for failing to safeguard Scottish interests while appeasing supporters who were keen on membership.

Emigration and the Lanarkshire economy

In 1962, Tom Fraser, Hamilton's Labour MP, and George Lawson, his neighbouring Motherwell colleague, wrote a confidential paper for the Labour Party highlighting the economic challenges faced in Lanarkshire and Scotland. Not only had Scotland's unemployment rate averaged twice that of Britain over the post-war period but Scotland's population growth had been slower. While the population of England and Wales grew by 5.3% between 1951 and 1961, growth in Scotland was only 1.6% despite higher Scottish birth rates. Scotland was losing people through emigration with an estimated loss of 25,000 people annually. The MPs warned, this 'emigration is of younger rather than of older Scots, and is of the skilled rather than of the unskilled'.[20] The economic boom that reached its peak in 1961 'never reached Scotland, but Scotland none-the-less was made to suffer the restrictions imposed in July 1961, when yet another balance of payments crisis hit Britain'.[21] They complained that the '"boundless prosperity" so often claimed for the country as a whole has been confined largely to a range of industries that have tended to settle overwhelmingly in the London-Birmingham conurbation'.[22]

These Lanarkshire MPs noted that Scotland had few of the industries that were required for the future and relied heavily on 'older declining industries'. They criticised the branch factory syndrome whereby central offices made the main decisions on investment and where research and development was concentrated, leaving branches with less security, fewer senior posts or opportunities. This would be a major theme in economic writings and journalism throughout the 1960s and 1970s.

Migration highlighted divergence on either side of the border. This had been a cause of grievance throughout the 20th century. This divergence was highlighted in two reports on consecutive days in the *Daily Express* in summer 1967. The first was an article by columnist Charles Graham entitled 'The Great Exodus' noting that 23,600 Scots had left the country in the previous six months. About one third moved to England or other parts of the UK with the remainder leaving the UK altogether. This was a 'shameful reflection on Government policies and a figure that casts a new and sharper light on the present unemployment total of 81,000'.[23] The following day the paper carried an article under the title 'COLOUR as this word captures the headlines' showing a map of England, identifying where immigrants had settled. The emphasis was on the new 'coloured' population of Britain. It acknowledged that a small immigrant community existed in Scotland – mainly Asians in Glasgow but the emphasis of the report was on the English conurbations.[24] There was much debate in Britain on 'New Commonwealth' immigrants. Enoch Powell's 'rivers of blood' speech in April 1968 would attract considerable attention leading to his dismissal from Edward Heath's front bench. Migration has long been framed differently on either side of the border and the SNP had long complained about the lack of opportunities driving Scots away.

The SNP's nationalism was markedly different from Powell's. In August 1966, the nationalist *Scots Independent* had carried an article, largely drawn from an earlier report in the *Scottish Daily Express*, featuring a 16 year old Asian Scot who had become dux of Scotland Street School in Glasgow. He had arrived eight years before knowing no English. He had clear views about Scottish politics. He told the *Express* that there was too little investment in Scotland's tourism industry and there was a need to rid Scotland of the 'image of a Scotsman as being a hairy moron'. He described himself as 80 per cent Scots, an early articulation of the idea of a dual identity Asian Scot. His support for a Scottish Parliament no doubt attracted the attention of the *Scots Independent*.

Labour dominance

Hamilton was thought to be one of Labour's safest seats following the 1966 general election. Tom Fraser had been MP since winning it in a by-election in 1943. The main parties had agreed a wartime pact agreeing that whichever party had won the seat at the previous election would be given a free run in any by-election. Fraser was returned with over 80 per cent of the vote against an Independent. Two years later, the pact created an opportunity for the SNP in neighbouring Motherwell. Minor parties were not involved in the agreement. Dr Robert McIntyre took the highly marginal seat from Labour with 51 per cent of the vote, only to lose it three months later at the 1945 general election. But there had been no SNP candidate in the field in Hamilton in 1943. At the 1945 election, Fraser won almost three-quarters of the votes in a straight contest with the Unionists. His lowest share of the vote was 66 per cent, won in 1959. This was the election when Labour began its rise to dominance in Scottish politics and the Tories started their gradual decline. The Hamilton result might seem aberrant but can be explained by the intervention of a third candidate, the first since a Communist had contested the seat in 1929. David Rollo, SNP treasurer and head of its Broadcasting Committee, stood for the SNP. The SNP was then on the fringe of Scottish politics and contested only five seats that year. Gordon Wilson, future SNP leader, has described David Rollo as the 'brain child' behind *Radio Free Scotland*, who brought a 'languid manner' and lateral thinking to the pirate radio station.[25]

Rollo was an able and intelligent candidate, described by contemporary local activists as someone who would have made a first class MP but struggled to gain the attention necessary to save his deposit. He spent his annual two weeks holiday in 1959 on the campaign trail. The local *Hamilton Advertiser* gave the candidate little coverage. Jack House, a well-known columnist with the *Evening Times*, followed Rollo for a day and carried a light-hearted piece referring to the 'calm sough' that the SNP candidate maintained throughout. One SNP activist noted that, when handing out leaflets outside *Hamilton Accies* football ground, someone had suggested that the SNP was 'worser nor ra IRA' in a reference to the nationalist campaign to blow up the EIIR pillar boxes. One of the national movements more newsworthy campaigns in the 1950s had been to challenge the designation of the new monarch as Elizabeth II on the grounds that the first Queen Elizabeth had not been Queen of Scots. This had included a legal challenge that resulted in an important legal case. In *MacCormick vs the Lord Advocate 1953*, John MacCormick, one of the founders of the SNP but by then a Liberal home ruler, challenged the legality of the Royal Titles Act 1953 in the Court of Session, Scotland's highest court. It was a legal defeat but, in true Scottish nationalist style, was seen as a famous political victory. Nationalists remember the comments of Lord President of the Court who noted in passing that the 'principle of unlimited sovereignty of Parliament is a distinctively English principle and has no counterpart in Scottish constitutional law'[26] but forget that the case was lost. A very different campaign was waged by a fringe who blew up a letter box in Edinburgh that attracted considerable attention and would haunt the conventional SNP. The post box campaign attracted considerable attention, a couple of folk songs were written and much myth-making followed. Myths do not require much basis in fact and the association of the movement with one blown up post box would embarrass the party.

Rollo had a consistent message: while 'social improvements' were important, he refused to get into a bidding game and saw self-government as the main issue, 'Adults did not want such bribes; they wanted responsibilities. In the same way, a nation should not be treated like a child by being promised bribes at election times. They should be promised responsibility, and when they accepted responsibility they would also get material benefits if they decided to run their own country in the interests of the Scottish people.'[27]

There was another Lanarkshire candidate arguing for home rule in 1959. Though the SNP had briefly held Motherwell, they had not contested it since 1950. However, David Murray, an Independent candidate, offered the same message as Rollo refusing to 'outbid the London parties with promises of material benefits' and reducing politics to the 'level of the kindergarten'.[28] Murray won even fewer votes than Rollo. The 1959 election in Lanarkshire had been overshadowed by a mining tragedy when 47 miners died at Auchengeich colliery, Chryston caused by an underground fire.[29] This would be the last election in which coal mining would play an important backdrop in an election in Lanarkshire.[30]

But while the SNP and home rulers did poorly, there was an underlying nationalist message to Tom Fraser's 1959 campaign. In an article in the *Evening Times*, Fraser noted that 900,000 jobs had been created in England over the previous eight years while 'Scotland showed no change' and he promised that Labour would 'redress the balance by ensuring that Scotland gets a fair share of Britain's jobs' by refusing development in 'congested places'.[31] Rollo won 6.2 per cent of the vote. He had not expected to get more than 2,000 votes but polled 2,586. The SNP averaged 11.3 per cent in the seats contested, making Hamilton its second poorest of the five seats contested. It was noted that, while Harold Macmillan had won a landslide, the Scots had 'said "No" to the Tories.'[32] The SNP continued to be active in Hamilton after 1959. The SNP back then struggled to get people to stand and Rollo had changed jobs and felt that his new employer would not look favourably upon him contesting a seat in 1964. The local party was also short of money and the poor 1959 result made contesting the seat unattractive.

MAKE YOUR VOTE COUNT

In Hamilton the Unionist candidate has no chance. If you vote Unionist you are wasting your vote.

If you vote Labour you may elect a member to sit on the Opposition benches with two hundred other Labour M.P.s But he will not be in the Government and will have to obey the decisions of a party which has turned its back on its promises of self-government and on most of the ideals of its pioneers.

Self-government has the support of the majority of the people of Scotland. A vote for Scotland is not a wasted vote. If you have the courage of your convictions on polling day we can, together, end the stranglehold which Westminster has on our country.

DON'T GIRN—VOTE!

Too many of us complain about the injustices done to Scotland—and then go and vote for one or other of the parties who are responsible for these injustices. Anyone who votes for the Labour or Unionist parties has lost the right to complain. One has proved itself as bad as the other. Unless we put our country before these parties we shall continue to have high unemployment, high emigration, lack of industry and opportunity, and all the other things which result from Westminster control.

PROVINCE OR NATION

The Scottish National Party says that Scotland is a nation—and not a region or province like an English county. We want a government in Scotland with the same amount of power as the governments of Canada, Australia or New Zealand.

SELF-GOVERNMENT MEANS SELF-RESPECT

When a nation loses the power to govern itself it loses its self-respect. Materially and mentally it becomes provincial. Its people feel no responsibility for the community in which they live.

The greatest benefits from self-government will not be material. There will be the feeling of belonging to a community, the restoration of responsibility and the focus given by the government to the creative abilities and enterprise at present being stifled by provincialism and remote control.

INDUSTRY AND ECONOMICS

Scotland in the past produced world-famous scientists and engineers. Now they have to go outside Scotland to find scope for their talents. They probably have jobs in Government establishments in the South of England or in Government-aided industries in the English Midlands maintained with the help of Scottish taxes.

The first economic duty of a Scottish government would be to use our taxes in our own country to set up research and development establishments and to promote and help new science-based and consumer-goods industries. We have the money and we have the men to do it.

SOCIAL SERVICES

It is easy to make promises. All the parties do it. Bigger pensions, more hospitals, and so on. But it is only a matter of commonsense that Scotland, with her own government, could keep up the present standard and improve it where necessary.

YOUR PART IN SCOTLAND'S FUTURE

Under self-government the running of Scotland will be in YOUR hands. YOUR ideas about what should be done and how it should be done will be just as important as mine or anyone else's. What I am asking you to do now is to give me the authority of your vote to demand that the government of Scotland be returned to the people of Scotland—to you!

HAMILTON CAN SHOW THE WAY

Scotland is waiting for a lead. You can give that lead on polling day. It needs only one S.N.P. candidate to be returned. As soon as that happens, Scotland would re-awake. It will happen. You can make it happen in Hamilton. If you do, I shall do my best to be worthy of your trust.

Yours sincerely,

DAVID ROLLO.

David Rollo's 1959 Election Address.

It was back to two party contests in 1964 and 1966 in Hamilton and Fraser won 71 per cent on each occasion. Labour was in the ascendant both in Scotland and across Britain. Harold Wilson became Prime Minister with a four seat overall majority in 1964 and extended that with a comfortable 96 seat overall majority after calling an election only 17 months later. Labour came closer to winning an overall majority of votes (49.84 per cent) in Scotland in 1966 than at any other election and it also had a very good result in England, not far short of its Scottish share.

Religion

An early study of Scottish politics identified a significant correlation between religion and voting in some parts of Scotland. Catholics were disproportionately more likely to vote Labour and Protestants to vote Unionist.[33] The Conservative Party had changed its name to

Scottish Unionist Party in 1912 in an effort to widen its appeal and drop what would now be called a toxic brand. This Unionism was not the Anglo-Scottish unionism, which was not then under threat, but union with Ireland. The Scottish Unionist Party managed to secure the support of a substantial proportion of working class Protestants who wanted to align themselves with their co-religionists in Northern Ireland. There were considerable links between Scotland, especially west central Scotland, and Ireland with flows of migrants both ways over generations. Irish nationalism had its staunch supporters and opponents in Scotland willing to lend support to the cause at the ballot box.

Conservative acquired negative connotations in 19th century Scotland and the prospect of aligning the party with unionism then had an obvious appeal. But this appeal diminished over time. By the early 1960s, it sounded anachronistic in much of Scotland and debates inside the party pointed towards a break with the past.[34] The modernisation of society (discussed below) was thought to make particularist messages increasingly irrelevant. From this perspective, the Scottish *Unionist* Party seemed an antediluvian throw-back. If the party wanted to remain relevant, it needed to change its name. In 1965, the party was rebadged as the Scottish Conservative and Unionist Party and became more closely aligned with the party in England. This was an attempt to modernise the party. The problem was that there were sections of Scottish society stuck in the past.

Hamilton lay in a part of Scotland that had long been associated with sectarianism. Larkhall was a bastion of Orange support with strong links with Northern Ireland. In the 1960s, Ian Paisley was becoming a well-known figure beyond his Northern Ireland base. A rally in Hamilton town hall addressed by Paisley in March 1967 attracted considerable attention. Controversy followed Paisley across the North Channel. The burgh chamberlain, in charge of hall bookings, banned Larkhall Rising Star Flute Band from playing pipes and drums at the rally, provoking the Glasgow Scottish Amateur Flue

Band Association to take legal advice with a view to suing Hamilton Town council for the £20 loss of earnings.[35] The Paisley meeting was a sell-out when about 10,000 Orangemen from Hamilton, Motherwell and Larkhall applied for tickets in a hall with a capacity of under 1,500.

An editorial in the local paper was clear, 'We stand by the conviction that everything that tends to perpetuate this religious division is hurtful to the life of our country... Mr Paisley is flogging a dead horse'[36] but gave a full report of Paisley's speech, 'all good-natured bigotry sprinkled liberally, if incongruously, with hallelujahs, amens and praise the Lords'.[37] Paisley spoke against membership of the European Economic Community, maintaining that the Treaty of Rome was 'definitely a religious document'.[38] His loyalism had been challenged. As he said, 'I hung my head in shame when the Queen went to see the Pope, veiled in black. When the throne of Britain flirts with Rome, it's a sad, sad day.'[39] Ewing and Paisley would both serve in the Commons and later in the European Parliament together. Though they had very different politics and backgrounds, Ewing developed good relations with Paisley.

The Scottish Catholic population benefited from a form of multicultural education policy that allowed for state support for Catholic schools. Some people saw this as fuelling separateness and sectarianism while others viewed it as a means of allowing a largely poor immigrant (predominantly Irish) community to integrate without assimilation. But alongside this classic division within liberalism, there were voices who viewed Catholic schools as an outrageous subsidy for alien immigrants. Few issues provoked more letters in the local Lanarkshire press but one that the main parties chose to ignore. In late 1966, all seven MPs in Lanarkshire received a letter from Lanarkshire Protestant Action Committee, an Orange pressure group, seeking their views on denominational schools. Only Tom Fraser replied, perhaps because by this stage he knew he would not be standing again. His views were out of step with a key demographic in Labour's support, though would find strong support in parts of his constituency. Fraser's stated position was that he was 'against the segregation of schoolchildren according to the church to which their parents belong' whether or not these schools were financed by the public purse. But he warned against any move that might be seen as directed against one church in particular.[40]

The Sixties

It is easy when focusing on the SNP's rise in this period to ignore broader social, economic and political developments. There was a sense of ineluctable progress. Each generation expected to be better off than its predecessor. Precisely how these developments affected electoral politics in Scotland, and Hamilton in particular, is unclear but there can be little doubt that people would have been aware of these developments, especially Hamilton's relatively young constituents. The 'swinging sixties', the 'counter culture' and major challenges to existing social, economic and political orthodoxies were the backdrop against which the by-election took place.

The sixties are now recalled as the era of the permissive society with liberal and progressive attitudes on sex and gender. In March 1967, a Private Members Bill in the Commons sought to encourage local authorities to support family planning but the Scottish Secretary opposed its extension to Scotland on moral and constitutional grounds, the latter referring to his belief that such matters should be determined by his Government office and not by a Private Members Bill. The local Hamilton paper argued that while it was legitimate to oppose the measure on religious or moral grounds or, as they imagined, for fear of alienating part of Labour's Catholic support, politicians should be honest about their reasoning.[41] David Steel sponsored a private members bill in the Commons, with Government support, to reform the law on abortion. There was a heated debate on the matter. Scottish law on abortion had been considerably more liberal than that in England though the interpretation of the legislation varied across Scotland.[42]

Homosexual law reform was also underway during this period but the law that was passed did not extend to Scotland. Leo Abse, the Welsh MP who sponsored the legislation, deliberately excluded Scotland fearing that his own Scottish Labour colleagues would oppose the measure. Abse's 1965 motion to introduce a bill faced its main opposition from Scottish MPs. Roy Jenkins, as Home Secretary sympathetic to liberalisation, remarked at third reading that he could not see the logic in omitting Scotland 'unless the sponsors realised that if they included Scotland, all Scottish Members would descend in their wrath and vote solidly against the Bill.'[43] So while, the liberalisation agenda might have been a key feature of politics in the mid/late 1960s, it was not embraced in Scotland. Matters such as abortion and capital punishment came up regularly at public meetings but there was a tendency across the parties to evade these matters unless a candidate adopted a stridently different stance from others. If, as in the Hamilton by-election, there was broad consensus that these issues should be avoided, then it was difficult for campaigners to insinuate themselves and their issues into the campaign.

These changes along with the rise of youth culture provoked a backlash. Mary Whitehouse set up the National Viewers' and Listeners' Association in 1965 to complain about sex, violence and bad language on television. Her crusade brought her to Lanarkshire in May 1967 when she addressed a meeting in Motherwell Town Hall.[44] One of her targets was Mick Jagger whom she accused of using microphones in a lewd manner during his performances. Police had raided Keith Richards' house in February where they found drugs leading Jagger and Richards to be sentenced to prison in June. These were all matters well covered in the media, including the local press.

More prosaically but more immediately relevant to Hamilton was news that Marks and Spencer was opening a shop in the town.[45] There was something stirring. An *Observer* journalist profiling the by-election the weekend before the vote wrote that Hamilton 'used to be the centre of the Lanarkshire coalfield, 'Cradle of the British Labour Party'... Keir Hardie was born eight miles from here. But there was been another revolution here since then, and the Labour Party, the candidates it picks, and the men who pick them have not changed to match' and quoted the Tory candidate saying that Scotland was going through a 'major revolution'.[46] He may have exaggerated its extent in suggesting that there was a 'Scandinavian flavour to the new homes and the clean sky behind them and the blue-eyed children. It looks and feels and is behaving like a new Scotland.'

The historian Arthur Marwick identified economic security as the 'unique ingredient' that explained the factors contributing to the emergence and development of social and political movements in the 1960s and allowed for 'innovation and daring'.[47] There was a convergence underwriting innovation, daring and minimising risks. The rise in the number of teenagers alongside growing affluence and rapid economic growth combined with new ideologies and the birth of 'rock and roll' to create and expand different subcultures. Yet alongside this growing affluence and confidence were setbacks. Not everything was working out well for everyone. While the whole may be improving, this was relative and some places and people felt left behind. The combination of being part of a world that appeared to moving forward and changing fast while feeling held back may well have contributed to a febrile political atmosphere. Some people may have been attracted to new politics, others repelled.

This was the world in which old patterns of behaviour and established values would be challenged: class was less important, the embellishment was coming to the fore. There is no empirical evidence to link the development of Scottish nationalism to what was happening more widely in society and the economy in the 1960s but sufficient circumstantial evidence to note that the background against which political debate took place was changing.

Sub-state nationalisms

There had been an assumption in many quarters that modernisation – urbanisation, industrialisation, and secularisation – would lead to greater integration of societies and the erosion of local identities. The common academic view was that movements such as the Scottish national movement were doomed to become even less relevant and would fade away. Some scholars thought these processes were irreversible and that local identities were anti-modern.[48] But the opposite happened and evidence began to emerge of the assertion of such identities in the 1960s. The fact that these developments occurred in a number of liberal democracies suggested that they must have a common cause. There were signs of rumblings of nationalist movements in advanced liberal democracies, though this needs to be set alongside the stability and absence of such developments in most countries.

Scotland was not alone in experiencing a nationalist advance in the 1960s. Plaid Cymru, the 'Party of Wales', showed earlier signs of advance and a 'Quiet Revolution' was already underway in Quebec. Plaid Cymru was founded in 1925, before the SNP. Its support was concentrated in Welsh speaking areas which was its strength and weakness, allowing it to advance but limited its appeal. Its focus was on the preservation of the Welsh language and culture rather than Welsh self-government.[49] Despite these differences, the two parties were allies and would exchange delegations to party conferences. Plaid's electoral performances were similar to the SNP's in so far as each party was showing signs of strength in the early 1960s.

The SNP took vicarious pleasure when Gwynfor Evans won the Carmarthen by-election for Plaid in 1966. The SNP's candidate in Hamilton in 1959 had attended Plaid Summer Schools with his family on a number of occasions. The SNP were keen to invite the new Welsh MP to Scotland and Evans toured Scotland following this victory. Ewing, as Hamilton prospective candidate, and Evans shared a platform in Aberdeen in October 1966. Evans referred to his desire to see Wales take its seat at the United Nations between Venezuela and Yemen. Ewing attended Plaid's annual conference in Merioneth in August 1967, along with Hugh MacDonald and James Braid, and presented Evans with a basket of white heather.[50]

Conservative Central Office in London awakened to the threat of Welsh and Scottish nationalism following the Carmarthen by-election. A confidential paper written by Chris Patten, then of the Conservative Research Department, on 'Nationalism and regionalism' noted the 'recurrent fear of a rash of Celtic Orpingtons'. Scottish and Welsh nationalism were a 'political expression of a national grievance'. He described both Plaid Cymru and the SNP as 'fairly left wing', though noted the SNP's opposition to steel nationalisation as this involved centralisation. While noting that the SNP campaigned on emigration, he felt that the 'electorate does not often get worked up over an issue like emigration from Scotland'. He warned that his party 'sometimes gives the impression of being a predominantly English party, and it has recently ruled because of its political strength in England' which was 'often strengthened by candidate selection'. He also noted that the Tories had 'openly played for the Scottish and Welsh vote by stressing our support for some sort of administrative devolution' but the party had 'no individually nationalist appeal'.[51] British nationalists were awakening to the new challenge.

There were similar developments in other parts of the world. Long-standing grievances existed in French-speaking Quebec and a new nationalist movement emerged around this time. The 'Quiet Revolution' was a reference to a variety of changes in Quebec society and economy in the 1960s. This modernisation and industrialisation was pursued by the Liberal Government and included nationalising the electricity industry undermining an old traditional economic, social and political order. A by-product was increased Quebecois self-confidence leading to demands for greater Quebec self-government. In July 1967, De Gaulle caused consternation in Canada's capital with his '*Vive le Québec libre*' call from a balcony in Montreal and was forced to cut short his visit when Canadian Premier Lester Pearson attacked this 'unacceptable' interference in internal Canadian politics.[52] Even before the French President's diplomatic incident, the SNP had written to the Queen urging her to invite De Gaulle to visit Scotland in 1968 to mark the eighth centenary of the *Auld Alliance*. Strange bedfellows were emerging. The leader of western Europe's most centralised state was aligning himself with sub-state nationalism in Canada and pursued as an ally by Scottish nationalists.

One view was that these developments, as well as evidence from Brittany and elsewhere, represented a 'revolt against dogmatic centralism, against the passion for social uniformity'.[53] Others focused more on the organisation and ability to mobilise support demanding reforms. The likelihood is that both the environment and capacity to organise explain these developments, but a further matter needs to be taken into account. There was an existing sense of identity and distinctiveness able to be mobilised. The sense that Scotland was different was not in itself enough but was an essential prerequisite. There needed to be a sense that this distinctiveness was worth preserving, might be under threat or even needed to be extended to allow for constitutional reform of one form or another.

Intimations of unrest and the politics of optimism

Something was stirring in the early 1960s, though the evidence was far from conclusive. Success can be measured in seats won, relative to past performances or measured against expectations. In 1975, SNP national secretary Rosemary Hall noted how the party kept altering the way is measured success: membership totals, then number of candidates fielded before votes won and ultimately number of seats.[54] Had SNP members measured success in seats won then their persistence is difficult to explain, other than dedication to a cause or the social aspect of party membership in which friendships were developed which carry members through successive defeats. The party came close to contesting no seats in 1955 and joining the long list of forgotten fringe parties that litter electoral history. The party took comfort in being able to contest more seats in the 1960s, increasing its share of the vote even if from a very low base, and occasionally save a deposit.

Many later interpretations of Scottish politics identify by-election progress as evidence of the forward march of the SNP but these advances were limited and sporadic. Optimistic and idealistic party activists probably shared the same interpretation of later commentators who sought evidence of a trend towards the SNP, ignoring or finding an explanation for inconvenient results. The two by-elections that are most often cited by SNP activists and in the literature on the rise of the SNP prior to Hamilton are Glasgow Bridgeton in 1961 and West Lothian in 1962. But there were other by-elections and tests of SNP support.

The SNP fought none of the six Scottish by-elections during the 1955–59 Parliament, including three seats it would win in 1974. Glasgow Bridgeton in November 1961 was the first by-election the party had contested in nine years. Ian Macdonald, its candidate, was a 26-year-old Ayrshire farmer. There was little reason to believe that the SNP would do well in a poor urban seat with an Ayrshire farmer as candidate, especially with limited resources and few activists but Macdonald came third with 18 per cent of the vote. This was enough to convince him to give up farming and work full-time as SNP national organiser. Macdonald then spent considerable time and effort travelling around Scotland setting up branches of the party.

Seven months after Bridgeton, Billy Wolfe stood as SNP candidate in the West Lothian by-election against Tam Dalyell for Labour. This would be the first of seven occasions when Wolfe and Dalyell would confront each other in electoral battle, gaining a place in the *Guinness Book of Records* as the two candidates who confronted each other most often over consecutive elections. Dalyell went on to become a well-known MP and the West Lothian Question – the anomaly of MPs being unable to vote on matters that have been devolved while still able to vote on comparable matters where there has been no devolution – was named after Dalyell's constituency in recognition of his persistence in raising it. But in 1962, the choice of a baronet with an ancestral home in the constituency who had been chair of Cambridge University Conservatives seemed odd in a largely working class constituency. The local *West Lothian Courier* suggested that 'some of the old West Lothian disciples of Keir Hardie' would be 'birling in their graves'.[55] The SNP's focus on the shale oil industry tapped into local concerns. The combination of what was then perceived to be an odd choice of Labour candidate, an exceptional SNP candidate campaigning on local issues about which he knew more than his rival helped the SNP advance.

When the West Lothian by-election had been called, a young David Steel had organised a meeting at his father's manse in Linlithgow and invited well-known local accountant Billy Wolfe to stand as Liberal candidate but Wolfe had already agreed to stand for the SNP. The Liberals found a candidate but lost their deposit while Wolfe had the best SNP result in a generation providing him with a base of influence in his party. He came second, winning 23.3 per cent and while Dalyell won 50.9 per cent this was seen as a major advance for the nationalists. It was also the first Unionist lost deposit since a by-election in Paisley in 1920. Wolfe's campaign started early and focused on local issues. The *Scottish Daily Express* headline declared, 'Labour, Scot Nat triumph' and the paper described it as 'one of the weirdest by-election results ever' with the Scottish Nationalist coming 'sensationally second in the five-cornered contest'.[56]

But against these by-election advances were other inconvenient results for those seeking evidence of an ineluctable forward march. Five months after West Lothian, the SNP came fourth behind Labour, Tories and the Liberals with 11.1 per cent in Glasgow Woodside. A year later, SNP leader Arthur Donaldson failed to make much impact, winning only 7 per cent of the vote coming fourth in the Kinross and West Perthshire by-election which saw Alec Douglas-Home take up a seat in the Commons. The SNP vote was half that at the 1959 election in a packed field of candidates, including one of the co-founders of *Private Eye*, attracted to the by-election by the candidacy of the Prime Minister. Donaldson was deeply disappointed and the poor result led to a review of the party's structure by Gordon Wilson. In Dundee West in November 1963, the SNP again won just over 7 per cent of the vote. But if there was one piece of consistent evidence that the SNP was moving forward, however slowly and unevenly, it was its ability to contest these by-elections. The SNP had struggled to contest seats in general elections in the 1950s. Missing a by-election would be the exception after 1961 but being able to contest a by-election was a low bar. Most striking of all was the tendency for SNP activists to remember the advances, ignore the setbacks and very limited progress.

Organisational improvements

It is difficult to know the extent to which an efficient organisation makes a difference in electoral politics. Success requires more than slick organisation but a message that has potential appeal needs to reach its target audience. There are occasions when political support comes in an overwhelming wave making organisation largely irrelevant. But these occasions are rare. There are many more times when potential support fails to be realised due to a lack of good organisation. The importance of Bridgeton and West Lothian was not only the evidence of an SNP support base but the lessons learned. They also supplied routes into politics for Macdonald and Wolfe who brought organisational skills, energy and leadership that served the party well over the following years.

The key lessons the party took from these by-elections were that organisation was important and campaigning on local issues mattered. Building on a belief in latent but untapped support for the party, other key figures emerged who took the view that the party needed a more professional organisation and more money. Angus McGillveray, a painter and decorator from West Lothian, established the Alba Pools lottery in January 1965 which raised considerable sums for the party. The combination of Ian Macdonald as organiser and Angus McGillveray as fund raiser has been identified in one study as important in creating new capabilities.[57]

Major organisational reforms were introduced following a report by Gordon Wilson. Between 1962 and 1970, the party was 'transformed into a modern efficient mass political party.'[58] The party learned that it needed to be better prepared for elections, including by-elections. In May 1967, the SNP's Vice Chair for Organisation set out the procedures for by-elections. As soon as it became clear that there would be a by-election, key office holders were to be informed immediately and a meeting arranged to meet local party officials the following day in the constituency. The party's Electoral Planning Committee would assume responsibility at national level for any by-election and meet with necessary co-opted local members. It was emphasised that no publicity or comment 'of any kind' should be made without the sanction of the 'proper official'.[59] The SNP was becoming more professional and disciplined, though still not as much as its much better resourced opponents.

The number of branches and members expanded in this period. There were only 21 branches in the whole of Scotland in 1962. By the end of 1965 there were about 140 branches, 152 by August 1966. According to a party official, 'most sizeable towns' had a branch though new branch formations were tailing off and 13 of Scotland's 71 constituencies had no branches and three had no SNP organised presence at all.[60] By December 1966, there were 190 branches and almost all constituencies had an SNP organisation in place in 1967. Hamilton provided another boost and there were 472 branches by 1968. Amongst the new branches formed in 1966 was one in Blantyre in the Hamilton constituency which was given national executive approval in July.

SNP MEMBERSHIP 1962–68			
1962	2,000	1965 November	20,000
1963	4,000	1966	42,000
1964	8,000	1967	80,000
1965 June	16,000	1968	120,000

Source: Kellas, 'Scottish Nationalism', in David Butler and Michael Pinto-Duschinsky, *The British General Election of 1970*, Basingstoke, The Macmillan Press, 1971, p.459.

Ian Macdonald toured the country tapping into dormant support and setting up new branches. The rapidity with which the party grew between 1962 and 1968 was, as one subsequent study stated, 'almost legendary'.[61] It had fewer than 2,000 members at the start of the 1960s and was claiming to have over 100,000 by 1968, though this figure exaggerates actual membership as it represented the number of membership cards sold to branches, whether or not branches managed to convert them into actual members.[62] The 1966 SNP conference was attended by 600 delegates, double that of the previous year.

Party membership not only grew. It attracted some colourful interest. Robin Douglas-Home, nephew of the former Prime Minister, joined the party and offered to stand as a candidate expressing the view that he had 'no particular constituency in mind' and added a postscript, 'I know Ludo Kennedy well.'[63] Kennedy was known to be sympathetic but was still a well-known member of the Liberal Party. Home had recently divorced the model Sandra Paul, who later married future Conservative leader Michael Howard, and was involved in a relationship with Princess Margaret around this time. He was informed that 'there is a certain procedure which we follow' and he could not simply choose a seat.[64] Another person who joined was Harry Cousins, a Dunoon hotelier and brother of Frank Cousins, trade union leader who served as Harold Wilson's Minister for Technology. These members at least drew attention to the party and contributed to the sense that it was moving forward.

Liberals and SNP

The Liberals had been in decline from early in the 20th century. Liberals took heart when Ludovic Kennedy won 35.5 per cent for the party in the Rochdale by-election in 1958. It was their best by-election performance since 1945. A month later, the Liberals won Torrington in Devon. Party membership and confidence grew making it possible to contest almost twice as many seats in 1959 as it had in 1955, doubling its share of the vote. The number of Liberal councillors grew. The Orpington by-election in 1962 won by the Liberals was thought by many commentators to mark the start of a Liberal revival. It appeared that the hold that Labour and Conservatives had on British politics was weakening.

While there was evidence of increased 'third party'[65] support across Britain, there was a problem for these parties in Scotland. If voters were disillusioned with the two party system and inclined to vote for a third party, there was a danger that votes would be split. Both the Liberals and SNP offered different versions of home rule. This was acknowledged by some in each party. The SNP did not stand in a by-election in Paisley in 1961 where John Bannerman, a well-known rugby international and keen home ruler, took 41 per cent of the vote for the Liberals. There was no Liberal candidate in Glasgow Bridgeton later that year allowing the SNP to win 18 per cent and come close to overtaking the Unionist candidate for second place. An academic study of the 1964 British general election speculated that part of SNP support was a 'disguised Liberal vote', as the SNP tended to pick up in areas where the Liberals did not fight.[66] It might equally have been argued that the Scottish Liberal vote was a disguised SNP vote.

The idea of a pact or arrangement between the Liberals and SNP was debated in the early 1960s. While some senior Liberals were hostile to cooperating with the SNP, others were open to the idea including Jo Grimond, David Steel, John Bannerman, James Davidson and Alasdair Mackenzie.[67] Talks were sanctioned by the leaderships of the two parties and these took place in March 1963 but there was no progress. The Kinross and West Perthshire by-election was too great an opportunity for both parties to miss. The Liberal candidate had previously spoken in support of Arthur Donaldson, SNP leader and candidate, but decided to stand and came second, with the SNP losing its deposit.[68] Billy Wolfe, who had made progress for the SNP two years before in West Lothian, became convinced that an electoral pact was needed but was defeated inside his party. Instead, the SNP challenged the Liberals to prioritise self-government but the Liberals would not be dictated to by another party. Both parties stood in the Dumfriesshire by-election in December 1963. The Liberals just pipped the SNP for third place but both lost their deposits, well behind the Conservatives and Labour.

There was only one Scottish by-election in the short 1964–66 Parliament. The SNP decided not to stand a candidate in Roxburgh, Selkirk and Peebles, preferring to support Liberal candidate David Steel but Anthony J.C. Kerr, who would become a well-known SNP activist, stood as an Independent Nationalist. John MacCormick, one of the SNP's founders and a key figure in the late 1940s campaigns for home rule, had channelled his energies into the Liberals and was Liberal candidate in the Borders seat in 1959 while Tam Dalyell stood for Labour. David Steel picked up the Liberal baton in 1964. Kerr won only 411 votes and was expelled from the party for his efforts, though he was later re-admitted and would be one of its most active members. Steel had eaten into the Tory vote in 1964 and was well placed to take the seat and won just under 50 per cent. This reminds us that even if the SNP was not contesting seats everywhere, there were Liberal and occasional Labour home rulers who kept the idea of a Scottish Parliament alive but also that the electoral system discouraged a breakthrough for third parties.

The problem for each home rule party was that they might have much in common but they were fishing in the same pool for votes.

It was difficult enough for a third party to break through under the first-past-the-post electoral system but more so when it had a competitor. As each party gained ground, it assumed it did not need to share the glory with the other and lack of advance for either was thought to make a pact rather pointless. In the 1960s, the Liberals and SNP seemed natural allies, as much as any two parties in Scotland but a distancing would occur over time. Standing more candidates at each election was seen by the parties as a sign of progress. The SNP announced it intended to contest all seats in Scotland after the 1966 election thus ruling out a pact with the Liberals.

Pollok

A report on the state of the SNP's Glasgow constituencies in July 1965 suggested that Pollok was not likely to be fertile ground for the SNP. Some of the constituency's most active members had joined the neighbouring Cathcart branch leaving only four active members and £37 funds. Compared with other Glasgow constituencies, Pollok was rated below average in organisational, membership and funding terms. It was a marginal Labour-Tory seat at the 1966 general election. When the local Labour MP died at a time when the Labour Government faced a variety of challenges, it looked likely to change hands. Labour adopted local councillor Dick Douglas.[69] The Tory candidate was Esmond Wright, a Professor of History at Glasgow University and a 'media don' with considerable television experience which he put to good use as candidate. The SNP put up George Leslie, a vet. As Paula Somerville suggests, in the most detailed history of the SNP in this period, Leslie was not a high profile figure.[70] He did not have the name recognition of a sitting Labour councillor or that of a media don but he proved able, charismatic and energetic.

Pollok was the first SNP by-election in which a levy was imposed on branches and constituencies to ensure that adequate funds were available for the campaign. As the 1967 annual report of the party's vice chair for finance noted, this was 'in marked contrast to the great difficulties experienced in the by-elections which occurred before the 1964 general election'.[71] Lessons were being learned and national officer-bearers were keen to learn. Another lesson learned from Pollok was referred to in a resolution considered for the 1967 party conference. This noted that it would be 'extremely advantageous for the Party to form groups for the purpose of moving in immediately to any constituency where there is a by-election'.[72] The following month the Election Planning Committee reported that constituencies near Hamilton were being encouraged to get involved in the by-election rather than in a planned national canvassing drive and it was agreed that these constituencies would not be sent the canvassing material that others received.[73]

A report on the Pollok By-Election in June 1967 records complaints that there had been 'too few personnel' in the early part of the Pollok campaign and that when large numbers of members appeared they were not used effectively. Some branches in Glasgow had not helped, thinking that there would be enough helpers without them and branches from outside Glasgow were not coordinated. The worst aspect of the campaign was felt to have been the lack of liaison between headquarters and the seven units into which the constituency had been divided. But numbers increased as the date of the by-election approached and this meant that all houses were canvassed and about 60 per cent canvassed twice, three leaflets were delivered as well as the election address.[74] James Kellas, doyen of Scottish political studies, reflected on the Pollok campaign suggesting that it had been 'something new in Scotland's dreary electioneering: it deliberately imported American-style motorcades, drum majorettes, jazzy literature and an all-pervasive fly-posting.'[75] The SNP virtually took over the constituency.[76] The party took heart from public meetings that attracted 'middle-aged bourgeoisie types, who, a few short years ago, would not have looked sideways at one of our meetings' but gave George Leslie a 'thoughtful hearing.'[77] Television had been the main medium from which the public gained most information about politics since the 1959 general election.[78] Esmond Wright's 'ease in his own medium' discomfited his opponents, apart from the Communist candidate whose 'down-to-earth and couthy manner left a very good impression'. At this point, the SNP was uncertain how to prepare candidates for television.

The report concluded that the West Lothian by-election had marked the 'renaissance' of the SNP and Pollok marked 'our graduation to a new professionalism' and it recommended a series of steps to be taken as soon as it was known that a by-election would occur.[79] Branches and constituencies had been asked to pay a levy for the costs of the by-election, though SNP headquarters were still chasing branches for their contributions in June 1967 it was acknowledged that the levy was in 'marked contrast to the great difficulties experienced in by-elections before the 1964 General Election.'[80]

Esmond Wright won the seat for the Tories. A Liberal candidate stood, winning only 735 votes (1.9%), just ahead of the Communist candidate. Labour lost the seat and blamed the SNP, which won 28 per cent of the vote, just 1,185 behind Labour. It was a remarkable achievement, not least as it appeared on paper to have been a two-party contest in the previous year's general election with less than 2,000 votes in it. The SNP could easily have been squeezed out of contention. A key lesson learned from Pollok was that it was 'important to get going with full momentum' as soon as was decent, a point previously made by party officials.[81] What was different this time was that it was organisationally much more competent. Ian MacDonald agreed to draw up teams for each area so that activity could occur as necessary. Groups of activists would be organised geographically, headed by the National Organiser and operate for the duration of the by-election and include two or three speakers.[82] The party was gearing up in a way it had never done before.

Three days after the strong performance in Pollok, the SNP executive decided to abandon any pact with the Liberals while some

Liberals took the opposite view. Liberal activists Ludovic Kennedy and Michael Starforth called for an electoral pact with the SNP at the Scottish Liberal conference in May 1967, two months after Pollok. Starforth later joined the SNP. But there was strong opposition from Russell Johnston, who had been elected MP for Inverness in 1964, and George Mackie, who held Caithness and Sutherland between 1964 and 1966. Johnston attacked Grimond for visiting SNP headquarters and the Scottish Liberal executive voted 16–2 against a pact. The Liberals invited the SNP to put the Scottish national interest above party interest,[83] but Jo Grimond continued to make the case for cooperation. Having stepped down from the leadership in January 1967 and against the developing backdrop of SNP support, his views were marginalised.

Conclusion

The backdrop to the Hamilton by-election was one of socio-economic change. For some people this would have been exciting and welcome, and, for others, frightening and seen as unnecessary. Economic turbulence and rising expectations in life chances are likely to spill over into politics. Those more weakly aligned to traditional parties and values are more likely to be attracted to new social and political movements. The novelty of the SNP should not be overstated. It appeared to combine a mix of support for a deeply rooted identity with modern attitudes, but it was not just that society and the economy was creating new opportunities for parties and movements but the SNP itself was becoming more efficient. Over the course of a number of by-elections, it appeared to have real potential. And, of course, by-elections meant that voters were not in danger of toppling a Labour Government in favour of a Conservative Government.

CHAPTER TWO

The Campaign

> Sons of miners no longer followed 'faither doon the pit'. Spain replaced 'doon the watter' as the holiday destination. And housing estates replaced council schemes for the 'upwardly mobile' who once would have been socially ostracised as 'snobs'.[1]

> The [*Hamilton*] *Advertiser*'s opinion, voiced many weeks ago was that Labour would win by 5,000 votes. Our later editions will show if we were near the mark.[2]

> At Westminster only a belief in the incredible allows a win for Mrs Ewing, the nationalist candidate, though she is expected to beat the Conservative for second place.[3]

> Bookmakers' odds in Hamilton on election day:
>
> Labour, favourite at 10 to 1 on
> SNP, 5 to 1 against
> Conservatives, 33 to 1 against.[4]

Hamilton Profile

THE HAMILTON constituency was an 'L-shaped' seat lying to the south east of Glasgow taking in Blantyre, Larkhall and Stonehouse as well as Hamilton. The constituency consisted of the Hamilton Burgh and the electoral divisions of Hamilton, Larkhall East, Larkhall West, Dalserf, Stonefield, Blantyre and High Blantyre in Lanark County. It was a largely working class constituency with 68 per cent of the population living in council housing and only one in five houses owned by occupiers.

Around 70 per cent of adults were semi-skilled workers and 16 per cent were unskilled. About a third of households had a car and

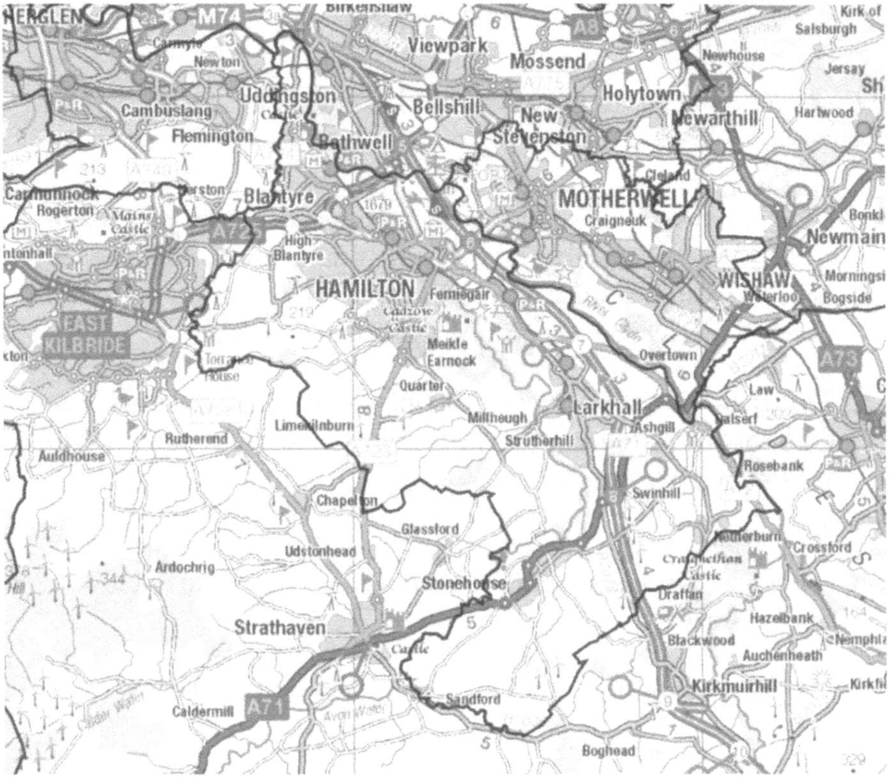

only 0.1 per cent were from the 'New Commonwealth'. Around 10 per cent were retired, 10 per cent were young voters and a further 10 per cent held professional or managerial positions.[5] But the composition of the working-class had changed from the days when coal was an important local industry. There were only 946 miners in the constituency and no functioning coal mines. Miners were easily outnumbered by employees of the local county council's 17 storey office block in Hamilton.[6] Hamilton was growing and the Burgh Surveyor was complaining about a 'land famine', with reports that the population was set to rise to 60,000 in 20 years.[7]

Proposals to create a new town in Stonehouse on the constituency's boundary was prominently covered in the media in the run-up to the by-election. The plan required the agreement of the Secretary of State for Scotland and reportedly involved creating a city of 124,000, a massive increase from an existing population of 10,000, to be completed by 2000. New towns had been a key element post-war planning. The 1946 *Clyde Valley Regional Plan* had argued that a quarter of a million Glaswegians should be moved to new towns. The first to be designated was East Kilbride in Lanarkshire, followed by Cumbernauld. New improved housing standards combined with the need for space for industrial development led the Scottish Office to turn again to new towns as an answer. Stonehouse was attractive given the ease of access to Glasgow.[8] Eventually, the idea was abandoned but in the late 1960s there was much excitement around the prospect.

1966 General Election and local elections

In March 1966, Harold Wilson won a landslide. The SNP put up 23 candidates, winning five per cent of the vote. Harry Rankin, SNP Treasurer, contested Lanark in the first three cornered election there since 1935 when Lord Dunglass (later Lord Home and still later Sir Alec Douglas-Home) held the seat against Labour and an ILP candidates. But Rankin lost his deposit with just over 10 per cent of the vote. In Rutherglen, the other Lanarkshire constituency contested by the SNP, the party won 6.4 per cent of the vote.

The SNP complained that they were excluded from television. A pirate radio station, *Radio Free Scotland* set out to overcome the dominance of the BBC[9] but its broadcasts lasted only a few minutes for very limited periods. Its impact was greater in press reports of its activities than its direct public reach. In 1966, the SNP was allotted five minutes on radio and television for contesting a fifth of seats in Scotland. Billy Wolfe made the case for the SNP. The SNP complained that they were not involved in discussions on allocation of broadcasting times. News reports, as the Nuffield election study noted, on television included a 'fleeting glance' at the SNP.[10] There were occasional references to the SNP in broadcasts – Independent Television news, for example, 'cast a fleeting glance at the Scottish and Welsh Nationalists'.[11] The SNP's first official party political broadcast came in 1965 and while this resulted in many applications for membership, it was unlikely to have made much impact – a few minutes of a broadcast would be lost in the hours of broadcasting which would have barely mentioned the party. But the party was becoming adept in communicating with the public given its limited resources, support and experience. Getting a broadcast was a sign that it had at least broken through a barrier.

The 1966 election was easily the SNP's best result until then. It retained 13 deposits and averaged 14.1 per cent in the seats contested. In West Lothian, the party won 35 per cent of the vote and Robert McIntyre won 26 per cent in Stirlingshire West. Coming only two years after the previous general election, the 1966 results convinced many in the party that it could contest all seats at the following election. It was now less than two per cent behind the Liberals, though the Liberals were much better at translating votes into seats, having won five of Scotland's 71 seats. There was optimism in the SNP ranks and there was much more party activity compared with a few years before. But there was little evidence that the SNP was on the verge of a breakthrough.

Local elections took place every year in Scotland in the 1960s, offering a constant stream of opportunities for the SNP. In 1963, Labour held 13 of the 15 council seats in Hamilton but the Unionists began picking up seats thereafter. There had been a 'strong swing to the Unionists' in Hamilton in the burgh elections in 1966.[12] Labour had eight councillors, there were six Unionists and one Independent when the elections were held in 1967. There were no SNP councillors in Hamilton though the party had contested local elections for some years. In February 1967, the local paper reported[13] that the SNP in Blantyre was planning to contest all three wards in the county and district elections. The Pollok by-election result gave the party confidence and more candidates were being put forward for local elections across Scotland. In March it was announced that the SNP would contest three wards in Hamilton and two in Burnbank. The SNP hoped to put up 100 candidates across Lanarkshire. The *Hamilton Advertiser* referred to the 'all-out Scottish National Party attack' which 'could produce startling results' after the 'shock of Pollok' though it noted that the SNP had 'never fared well in Hamilton'.[14] The paper suggested that the 'contests could well prove the most exciting ever'.[15] John McAteer, who would become Winnie Ewing's election agent, planned to stand again in Hamilton after polling 334 votes in a by-election the previous November. But in an indication of the kind of trouble ahead for the SNP, two nationalists competed against each other in one part of Lanarkshire. Winnie Ewing, by now well established as SNP prospective Parliamentary candidate, campaigned alongside the local government candidates in early 1967.

The SNP contested every seat but came bottom of the poll in each. Labour suffered losses in Lanarkshire, as across Scotland, in the town council elections but retained control of all county councils except East Kilbride. It did better in Larkhall where it helped oust Labour from control of the District Council and won a seat in Blantyre. It performed even better in the county council elections proving 'themselves a force to be reckoned with', according to the local paper.[16] There was a 'new sense of practical urgency which is obviously animating the party', ascribed to the dissatisfaction with past and present governments.[17]

A by-election for a seat on Glasgow Corporation in Glasgow Gorbals a week before the Hamilton generated considerable media interest and suggested a rise in support for the SNP but the party did not live up to its own hype. The SNP candidate was 26-year-old Alex Ewing, no relation to Winnie, who remained very active in the Hamilton by-election while campaigning for his own election. The Gorbals local by-election was interesting for the field of candidates that included Conservative candidate F.W. Craig, who would later become well known as the compiler of election statistics, and Jimmy

Wray, later to become Labour MP for a seat in Glasgow's east end, but then standing as an independent having fallen out with his party.[18] Labour held the seat with 39 per cent of the vote compared to the SNP's 28 per cent, double its share of the vote from May's elections, on a 30 per cent turnout.[19] On polling day, the *Glasgow Herald* maintained that it was impossible to predict the outcome with seven candidates standing though the paper was encouraging voters to protest against the Labour controlled local authority, heavily hinting that voting Conservative was the best means of doing so.[20] In the event, the SNP was the main channel of protest, with almost twice as many votes as the Tory. It signalled two key messages: voters wanted to express some dissatisfaction with Labour, but they were not inclined to vote Tory despite pressure from sections of the press.

Labour Government troubles

Harold Wilson's 'white heat of technology' rhetoric had helped Labour's return to power but created expectations that would be difficult to realise. The modernisation agenda soon looked tarnished. On 24 July, less than four months after the general election, Crossman described the 'destruction of the Wilson myth in the public eye' and the 'most dramatic decline any modern Prime Minister has suffered.'[21] The 1966 Labour victory felt distant within less than a year. In July 1967, Peggy Herbison resigned as Minister of Social Security attracting damaging front page headlines. Her 'bombshell resignation', as the *Daily Record* described it, was because she felt that the increase in family allowance was 'NOT BIG ENOUGH'. Described as 'loved and respected' and the 'wee Scotswoman with the heart of gold', the *Record* reported that she had been unhappy with the Government's measures to tackle poverty. The resignation took place less than four months before the by-election. Herbison had been MP for North Lanarkshire since 1945. Another local Lanarkshire Labour MP had fallen out with the leadership earlier in the year. George Lawson,

Motherwell MP, complained about being sacked as a whip because of disagreements with Labour's Chief Whip.[22]

Harold Wilson faced a series of rebellions from backbenchers leading to his warning that, 'every dog is allowed one bite, but a different view is taken of a dog that goes on biting all the time. He may not get his licence renewed when it falls due'.[23] But Constituency Labour Parties issued MPs with a 'licence' and they were often more sympathetic to the rebels than the Government. Sackings combined with criticisms undermined the Government's efforts. There were also reports of trouble at the top of the Labour Party in the run-up to the by-election. George Brown, Labour Foreign Secretary and Labour's Deputy Leader, had very publicly and loudly attacked Lord Thomson of Fleet at a dinner at the Savoy Hotel, London, two days before the election. Brown was unwell and had a history of erratic behaviour followed by much media speculation about his position in government. The impression was of a government that was in difficulty, if not disarray.

A debate was held in the Commons in early July on the Scottish economy, opened by Sir Keith Joseph, Conservative Shadow Minister for Labour and followed by Douglas Jay, President of the Board of Trade. The long-established pattern of the party in opposition playing the Scottish card to attack the Government was in evidence. Joseph accused the Labour Government of failing to ensure that Scotland received its share of the 'rising number of civil servants' and listed five main Government establishments that might have been set up in Scotland but had gone elsewhere: the Royal Mint in Cardiff; the National Computer Centre in Manchester; the Steel Corporation in London; the Land Commission in Newcastle; and the Vehicle Taxation Centre in Swansea.[24] Jay warned that there were 'strong natural forces working against us and there is a long way to go', recognising the challenges before the Government.[25] The main criticism was that Labour had inherited a booming economy and in 18 months had made little progress and that Willie Ross, as Secretary of State for

Scotland, had failed to ensure Scotland won its fair share of Government projects. It was a typical adversarial debate. One newspaper report described it as a 'piteously inadequate, fumbling performance in which Tory-Labour politicians demonstrated their own futility, and that of their bumbling policies'.[26]

In late August, Harold Wilson announced a major government reshuffle. He took charge of the Department of Economic Affairs, in a move interpreted by the *Glasgow Herald* as 'analogous to Prime Ministers combining responsibility for defence in time of war'.[27] This 'economic overlord' role highlighted the challenges facing his government. There was a fear that unemployment in Scotland might rise to over 100,000 in the winter, having reached 81,000 in July and with the highest unemployment rate for August in 27 years. Lanarkshire recorded the highest increases in Scotland in early summer. In late October 1967, Wilson paid a flying visit to Scotland, pledging to slash unemployment. He told journalists that Scottish jobless figures would be brought to 'near the national level by the end of the Parliament'.[28] The STUC general secretary called on Wilson to stop behaving like King Canute before the 'rising tide of unemployment engulfs' the government.[29]

Labour unrest also caused headaches for Wilson's Government. Disputes in London and at the Liverpool docks saw more than 15,000 dockers go on unofficial strike in 1967, with an impact on international trade and Britain's balance of payments. Back then, the balance of payments assumed importance as an economic indicator that unemployment and inflation would later assume. A strike by busmen added to the sense that industrial relations were deteriorating. Bus passengers faced 'chaos', according to the press, due to a voluntary overtime ban in some parts of Scotland with the threat of an all-out strike averted in Glasgow at the end of October 1967. Given the low proportion of car ownership in parts of Scotland, such as Hamilton, this threat would have serious implications for people travelling to and from work and for pleasure. But while Labour was in trouble, the Conservative Opposition had its own problems. Edward Heath, elected leader in 1965, was attacked by party colleagues with calls for a change of leadership during this period.

Mood for change

In September 1967, the *Daily Record* carried articles based on a book by Max Nicholson.[30] Nicholson was highly respected across parties. He had served as a senior civil servant with Labour Deputy Prime Minister Herbert Morrison under Attlee. William Waldegrave, who served in Margaret Thatcher's cabinet, described Nicholson as the 'father of British environmentalism', as founder of the Nature Conservancy and World Worldlife Fund, and 'godfather of the British town and country planning system' and noted that Nicholson turned down a knighthood offered by Thatcher.[31] Nicholson's 1967 book was given extensive and sympathetic coverage in the press for its criticism of the civil service. It had a mixed reception in Government. Harold Lever, Financial Secretary to the Treasury, offered a 'violent attack' on Nicholson on radio, according to Cabinet Minister Richard Crossman. Crossman was convinced that the Treasury's senior civil servants had put his Labour colleague up to attacking Nicholson. He thought that Nicholson should get a medal for his 'wonderful work' which was a 'tremendous onslaught on the civil service and, in particular, on the mandarin mind'.[32]

Nicholson tapped into a prevalent view at the time that government was over-centralised, bureaucratic, and controlled by an Oxbridge educated elite. Wilson had established a Royal Commission on the Civil Service in early 1966 to examine the structure, recruitment and management, including training, of the civil service as part of the 'modernisation' of government. Nicholson's thinking was in the vein of Labour modernisers but the application of his thinking to Scotland had nationalist overtones. The articles in the *Record* were written by Michael Grieve, the son of the nationalist/

Communist poet Hugh MacDiarmid[33] who would ghost write Winnie Ewing's columns in the paper after her election to Parliament.[34] Nicholson was quoted saying that he would 'not vote for any candidate who did not pledge himself [sic.] to fight for a Scottish Parliament' in an article by Grieve entitled 'Scotland the Tame'.[35] Nicholson's critique focused on the 'untrammelled control' of Scottish Office civil servants with their 'passion for centralisation' and suggested that while Scots sang 'Scotland the Brave', they behaved like 'Scotland the Tame'.[36] It is unclear the extent to which this was Grieve or Nicholson talking, but the central thesis was certainly a key theme in the latter's book and the mood for modernisation was in tune with the message the SNP were pushing. Few of Hamilton's voters will have read the book but many may have been aware of the broad critique reported in the press. The sense that bureaucrats ran the show who were out of touch with the public was part of the *Zeitgeist*.

Rumours of impending by-election

Rumours started to circulate of an impending by-election in Hamilton well over a year before it was called. Tom Fraser, incumbent Labour MP, had been a junior Scottish Office Minister in Attlee's post-war Labour Government and Minister of Transport under Harold Wilson. As Transport Minister he had introduced the 70 mph speed limit on motorways and authorised the closure of over a thousand miles of railway lines on the recommendation of the Beeching Report. He was moved to the backbenches in December 1965 when he was 54 and knew his career as a Minister was over but he was not ready to retire nor give up public service. Rumours circulated within weeks of the 1966 general election that he might be offered a position as head of a public body, possible chair of the South of Scotland Electric Board, and stand down from Parliament.

In April 1966, Russell Thomson, a Midlothian SNP activist who had produced a party booklet, *How to Build up Your Constituency*, sent a note to leading members of the party discussing the possibility of a by-election in Hamilton. Thomson requested a report from local party members in Hamilton. There were then two branches. Clydesdale had 27 members, including nine who were active, with about £11 in the bank. Hamilton branch had 85 members, including 25 activists, and had about £150 in the bank. Eight of the Hamilton branch lived in Larkhall. It was clear that, in the event of a by-election, the party's headquarters would have to take on the cost and there was little likelihood that constituencies which had only just fought a general election would be able to help much financially. In August 1966, SNP HQ agreed to make available £200 for a by-election in Hamilton. It was suggested that branches within 45 minutes of Hamilton should be asked to provide teams of activists and that as soon as the burgh elections were over, all branches would be encouraged to supply teams to start canvassing the constituency. Thomson suggested that a candidate should be adopted 'without delay and get him [sic] known in the area (meetings, coffee mornings etc.)'.[37] A couple of potential candidates were named: J. Muirhead who worked with Atholl Houses and W. Clark of the Hamilton branch.[38] His description of the constituency was clearly based on some out of date information as he listed three local papers, two of which were no longer in circulation, highlighting the importance of local intelligence.

Hamilton constituency SNP formally chose Winnie Ewing on 20 July 1966, the day before Gwynfor Evans took his seat in the Commons after winning Carmarthen for Plaid Cymru, though it took about a month for Hamilton SNP to inform headquarters. This was not an attempt to ignore SNP HQ but simply a lack of awareness of procedures. Procedures were important to Gordon Wilson, the party's National Secretary. In a letter to Robert McIntyre in early August 1966, Wilson informed the SNP President that Winnie Ewing, a lawyer colleague, had told him she would be formally adopted as prospective parliamentary candidate on 8 August, 'I have the greatest respect for Mrs Ewing and would support her nomination' but he could not recall the national executive committee approving her 'which is the normal procedure' and urged that this be dealt with at the next NEC meeting.[39]

The prospect of an imminent by-election was receding so there was less urgency. In August 1966, the SNP chairman felt that any 'voluntary by-elections' planned by Labour would be postponed, given the dangers of defeat following Gwynfor Evans' victory. But Donaldson warned the party's National Council in September that a by-election somewhere is 'not likely to be long delayed' with an opportunity 'no matter how "safe" the seat may have been in the past'.[40] Other reports from senior party officials urged that preparations be made for a by-election, including one from the Vice Chair for Finance who was keen to ensure that money was available. The Vice Chair for Organisation presented an updated report on Hamilton to a meeting of the national executive in August. By this stage, Hamilton had four SNP branches: Hamilton, Larkhall, Blantyre and Clydesdale. Another in High Blantyre would be formed. But Hamilton did not yet have a constituency association. Party HQ organised a meeting in Hamilton to offer assistance and arrange an adoption meeting for the candidate. Having four branches was then unusual. Only three other constituencies in Scotland had four branches and most had only one, though neighbouring Lanark had six branches.[41]

Ewing had two formal adoption meetings, one in September 1966 as prospective parliamentary candidate, and another a year later as candidate.[42] At her first adoption meeting, she outlined her thinking. She argued for 'home rule' which, she maintained, was at the 'root of every aspect of life and must come first' and listed 'six sorry chapters of misrule': development of Scotland's resources; crippling emigration; lack of fuel and transport policies; Scotland's housing needs; unemployment; and economic policies addressing Scotland's specific needs.[43]

John McAteer

At a meeting of the SNP's Organisation Committee in August 1966, Jimmy Braid,[44] Provost of St Monans in Fife, suggested that responsibility for the by-election should 'be more than local' but Ian Macdonald felt that the local organisation was 'capable of running the election'[45] and reported that John McAteer would be the election agent. McAteer proved to be an indispensable local organiser. Gordon Wilson, then National Secretary, later described how McAteer ran a 'taut, well-organised campaign supported by thousands of supporters'.[46] He was a key figure deserving recognition for his considerable part in the by-election and subsequent SNP successes. McAteer was principal technical teacher at Saint Saviour's Catholic school in Bellshill after joining the SNP in the 1950s, when he was training to be a teacher, along with his friend John Byrne. Byrne was an art teacher who sought to improve the SNP's drab posters and one of the new blood bringing talents and ideas into the party. The impact of people like McAteer and Byrne would soon be felt. McAteer moved to Hamilton and, from 1962 until the by-election, stood as SNP candidate in local elections. In May 1967, he stood again but came bottom of the poll, in common with all other SNP candidates in Hamilton, with 16 per cent of the vote.

Like many political activists in their early 30s, he combined political activism with bringing up a young family. It became a joke amongst his friends that each election address would simply be amended to add reference to the latest addition to his family. His friend Hugh MacDonald, who played a key active part in the by-election,[47] described John McAteer's role in an obituary published in the *Scots Independent*:

> John was architect of the organisational and political strategy that shattered the Labour establishment within its fortress of Hamilton. In terms of sheer professionalism it was the finest piece of organisation and deployment of forces that the National Party has witnessed.

> He assembled a team of battle-proven activists with just the right injection of new blood to set the whole campaign going. With John McAteer as election agent and Winnie Ewing as candidate, the chemistry, or maybe it was the alchemy, was just right.[48]

In late 1966, McAteer was on the SNP candidates list and a member of the SNP national executive committee. His skilful management of the Hamilton campaign ensured a political career but not one that he might have anticipated in the mid-1960s. McAteer replaced Ian Macdonald as national organiser in December 1968 when Macdonald stood aside to concentrate on seeking a parliamentary career.[49] It is easy – and understandable – to focus on the successful politician, but as Winnie Ewing always insisted, she owed her victory to remarkable local activists. In September 1966, well before the by-election took off properly, she wrote to Robert McIntyre to thank him for sharing a platform with her and expressed delight at the support of the local party, expressing the view that it was 'obvious that I am very fortunate in having such local enthusiasm'.[50] Fifty years later she recalled the central role John McAteer had played.

There was a camaraderie in the Hamilton campaign that created friendships, easily missed when viewing politics from a distance of time or space. An intriguing feature of much political activism is the willingness of people to work hard for a party or cause when evidence points against success. A combination of a belief in the cause and a sense of community develop amongst like-minded individuals. Faith may exist that even if the immediate signs do not augur well, foundations are being laid for more propitious times. In his obituary of McAteer, Hugh MacDonald noted that it is 'easy to do a good job when you have excellent tools and good back-up' but John McAteer's achievement, first evident in Hamilton, was that he 'managed to execute the job with the barest necessities and least cost to the party.'[51] McAteer was once heard to remark that, 'This party punishes you'. But it was self-inflicted. When he became election agent, he approached his local education authority to get time off work but this was rejected.

He was told that if he took time off then he would not have a job back to return to. This was a bureaucratic rather than a party political reaction. His sanguine view that they would not refuse him his job proved correct, perhaps due to the high-profile result, but worried his wife.[52]

John McAteer went on to contribute massively to the SNP as National Organiser. He oversaw the SNP's 1970 general election campaign which proved disappointing but was nonetheless a step forward. He was heavily involved in November 1973 when Margo MacDonald from Hamilton was the SNP victor in the Glasgow Govan by-election. Within months, he was organising the party's general election campaign which saw it win seven seats in February 1974 and again in October when it won 11 seats with 30 per cent of the vote. He died aged 44 in February 1977. Billy Wolfe, SNP chair, described him as a 'saintly man' and almost a thousand people attended his funeral.

Winifred Ewing

In general elections, the candidate in any constituency is largely sheltered from the national campaign that dominates the news media. In a by-election, the candidate is exposed to an extent more comparable to that of leading party figures in general elections. This exposure may attract candidates keen on a national platform early in their career while party apparatchiks might seek a safe berth in the relative anonymity of a general election. Weak candidates can be carried along by a national tide, just as strong candidates can suffer when the tide ebbs. But there is no place for a weak candidate to hide in a by-election. The long campaign gave her exposure that would not normally be available in most by-elections. That familiarity would be a major advantage for the SNP. Though she would soon be known as Winnie, the SNP candidate was usually referred more formally as Winifred Ewing until after her election.

Ewing was an exceptional candidate with a remarkable background. Her father had been an Independent Labour Party supporter. Her approach to life appears to have been reflected in her attitude to the campaign: anything was possible if you believed it could be achieved. It was less arrogance than an almost innocent self-belief and a strong belief in others. She had many options before her at the point when she agreed to stand for Parliament. She studied Law at Glasgow University and The Hague Academy of International Law, spoke fluent Dutch and had been Secretary of the Glasgow Bar of Lawyers for four years at the time of the by-election as well as studying for the English Bar having been admitted to Gray's Inn. She was lecturing in law and was considering whether to pursue an academic career. Her European experience in the 1950s imbued her with a keen sense of European politics and recent history. Her autobiography refers to a relationship with a German lawyer and former Luftwaffe pilot, remarkable for the time, and records an evening in the 1950s listening to Willy Brandt speaking about the future of Europe. Her European identity, as much as her Scottish identity, was emotional and idealistic. She was vivacious and highly sociable. Her wide circle of friends proved deeply loyal and very supportive during the by-election and beyond. It is impossible to know where she might have ended up had she not won Hamilton or not become involved in politics having won and lost the seat but there seems little doubt that someone with her intellect, interpersonal skills and self-belief would have shone whatever path she had chosen.

While she set out to win and took the campaign very seriously, Winnie Ewing had little involvement with the SNP prior to being adopted as candidate. She and her husband Stewart were supporters but busy professional lives and a young family limited what they could do. However, she had come to the attention of party leaders. A meeting of the Election Committee in July 1962 considered possible parliamentary candidates for the next election. This was a wish list which included some assumed to be sympathetic as well as some members, including Donald Stewart of Stornoway, sociologist Dr John Highet, Magnus Magnusson, playwright Robert Kemp, Winifred Ewing and Gordon Wilson.[53]

Tam Dalyell refers to her being a member of Glasgow University Labour Club, which would have been understandable given the strong bond with her father and his Independent Labour Party (ILP) support,[54] but is inaccurate. Her older sister Jean was a Labour Party member and Jean's husband James Forsyth was unsuccessful Labour candidate in Edinburgh South on three occasions in the 1950s including a by-election in 1957. Dalyell maintained that a 'major factor in the SNP's success was the attractiveness – both in a political and physical sense – of their candidate'.[55] James Halliday, who chaired the SNP from 1956 to 1960, was a contemporary of Winnie Woodburn, as she was then called, at Glasgow University and recalls 'exchanging mere courtesies' but did not recall her attending Glasgow University Scottish Nationalist Association (GUSNA) meetings.[56] She came to the notice of senior figures largely through her career as a lawyer. One of her students enthused about her to the party leadership. By this stage Ewing was married and it took time for Halliday to realise that Winnie Ewing, the inspirational law lecturer, was Winnie Woodburn, with whom he had been acquainted in his days at Glasgow University. In his memoir, Halliday tells how 20 years after exchanging pleasantries at university, he met her and Stewart Ewing at a dinner honouring Tom Gibson, a leading SNP figure.[57] She was occasionally active but family and career commitments limited what she could do. Her first public speech for the SNP was in a by-election in Stirlingshire which brought her to the attention of Robert McIntyre. She attended her local Cathcart branch meetings and various SNP functions but did not seek senior party positions.

In 2011, Ewing returned to Hamilton to open the constituency office of the recently elected Member of the Scottish Parliament for Hamilton, Larkhall and Stonehouse. This was the first time Hamilton had returned a SNP member in a Parliamentary election since 1967.

During what the local paper described as an 'emotional return', Ewing recalled how she had been adopted for the by-election. Some SNP members from Hamilton came to her Glasgow Southside home when rumours circulated that a by-election was likely. She was reluctant to stand but was provoked when her husband told her she was wasting her time as local members were bound to choose one of the men also consideration.[58] The other potential (male) candidates fell by the way and she emerged as the candidate unopposed with strong support locally and nationally. By the time she was formally selected it looked as if the by-election might not occur after all, so it was anticipated that there were would be a long campaign leading up to the next general election.

Her gender has been the focus of attention in much subsequent commentary. The standard observation was that she was a novelty standing in male-dominated Lanarkshire politics. In fact, while there were few women politicians in Scotland, Lanarkshire was then represented in Parliament by two women. Peggy Herbison in North Lanarkshire had been elected and Judith Hart in Lanark was on Labour's front bench. Ewing did not shy away from her gender. In addressing a monthly meeting of the Larkhall Professional and Business Men before the by-election, she avoided making an overtly partisan speech and spoke about Scots law and included a section addressed to the wives of members who were present, outlining their rights under Scots law.[59]

There is invariably much speculation on whether any female politician is a feminist, measured in a variety of ways. The most basic way has been whether the politician describes herself as a feminist, offers support to women in public and political life, campaigns on various issues, or contributes to the advancement of women. The yardstick for women politicians on women's advancement is invariably much higher than for men. Male politicians are accredited for the merest contribution on any of the measures mentioned while women are usually expected to have performed strongly on each. In an interview days after winning the by-election, Ewing was asked: 'what sort of woman would you say you are?' She replied, 'A feminist. I believe that a woman can do just as well as a man, and sometimes even better. I've been asked why I stood for Parliament and not my husband, who is also wholeheartedly nationalist. The answer to that lies, I think, in our professions. He's an accountant, a sort of backroom man who keeps everything running smoothly. I'm a solicitor who works in the harsh limelight of Glasgow Sheriff Court and I'm used to making myself heard in public. Therefore, it seems more natural for me to stand for Parliament.'[60] It is notable that she described herself as a feminist at this time and would use the platform offered as a Parliamentary candidate to take the case for women's rights where it was not always expected or, probably, appreciated.

Ewing had considerable support behind the scenes. Her husband Stewart had not only encouraged her to stand after that initial provocation but is mentioned frequently by those who were close to the campaign for giving strong support. This was remarkable given his generation and background. His faith in his wife's abilities or at least his way of showing support included placing a bet of £100 on her victory. Ewing allowed herself a much more modest flutter. A wide range of friends, not all politically active, helped in assorted ways during the by-election and thereafter.

Winnie Ewing was not well known to local party activists or the SNP nationally when she was adopted. But her standing in the SNP changed from the moment of her adoption. She forged a strong bond with Robert McIntyre from the start that lasted until his death in 1998. In a letter to McIntyre in early September 1966, Ewing thanked him for his support at her public adoption as prospective candidate and offered an insight that she did not often share with others. She admitted it had been an 'ordeal' being on a public platform but was 'enormously cheered' to have him sitting with her.[61] She was elected in fourth place to the SNP's national executive committee in June 1967, no doubt largely because she was the by-election candidate. George Leslie, who had performed strongly in the Pollok by-election came top.[62]

Three days before polling day, the *Scottish Daily Express* sent Lady Lothian, one of its leading columnists, to Hamilton. Lothian was a champion of various causes, especially women, and had founded the Women of the Year Lunches at London's Savoy Hotel a decade before. She was impressed by Ewing, expressing regret that she had to leave Ewing after the interview and described the prospective MP as a woman to make an impact in any party and a 'fantastic asset to the SNP.' Having attended each party's morning press conferences, Lothian felt that the two main parties were 'stupid' in their reaction to the SNP in hoping that it might go away if ignored. It was absurd, she felt, to dismiss its support as a protest vote. Her perspective might have influenced her son Michael Ancram, an ambitious young Scottish Tory. Ancram would become the most active member of the Thistle group, a Scottish Tory ginger group set up in 1967, which advocated devolution and greater emphasis on Scottish dimension in Tory politics including party reforms, though he led the anti-devolution campaign in the 1997 referendum.

Labour selection

Labour might have come close to winning a majority of all votes cast in Scotland in 1966 but the party was almost moribund in many seats including some where its support was strongest. It had few full-time agents. Outside Glasgow and Dundee, the party had only four full-time agents in Scottish constituencies and was dependent on volunteers. A 'rough estimate' of Labour's Scottish contribution to the party's London coffers was put at £34,000 (the equivalent of £605,000 in 2017). Its Scottish membership, including trade union members, was 697,062 but many of these 'members' would have been unaware they were included. Individual fee-paying membership registered with local parties was 78,858 though a much smaller

VOTE... EWING...
FOR A CHANGE VOTE EWING SCOTTISH NATIONAL PARTY
WILSON'S ADVICE TO HIS PERFORMING POOCHES
"Every dog is allowed one bite. But a different view is taken of a dog who bites all the time. If the dog bites because he is vicious something happens to the dog. He may not get his licence renewed when it falls due."
SWINGS HAMILTON TO THE
SNP

VOTE EWING
VOTE EWING
SNP

scotland v.
whitehall
Winifred Ewing's
BLACK
BOOK
4/-

VOTE....EW
EWING
SCOT
CANDI

VOTE
EWING
VOTE
EWING

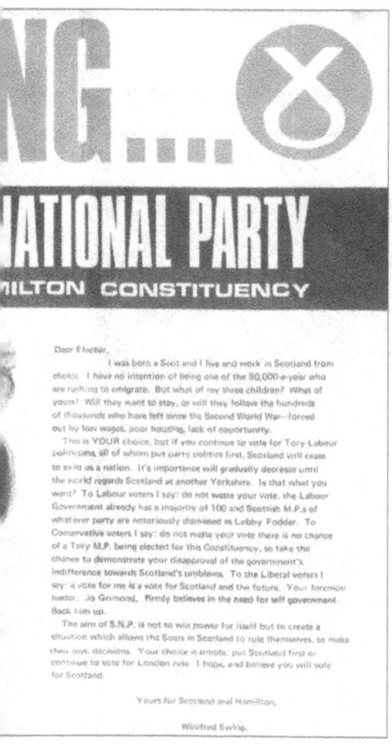
NG....
IATIONAL PARTY
ILTON CONSTITUENCY
Dear Elector,
I was born a Scot and I live and work in Scotland from choice. I have no intention of being one of the 50,000-a-year who are rushing to emigrate. But what of my three children? What of yours? Will they want to stay, or will they follow the hundreds of thousands who have left since the Second World War—forced out by low wages, poor housing, lack of opportunity.
This is YOUR choice, but if you continue to vote for Tory-Labour politicians, all of whom put party politics first, Scotland will cease to exist as a nation. It's importance will gradually decrease until the world regards Scotland as another Yorkshire. Is that what you want? To Labour voters I say: do not waste your vote, the Labour Government already has a majority of 100 and Scottish M.P.s of whatever party are notoriously dismissed as Lobby Fodder. To Conservative voters I say: do not waste your vote there is no chance of a Tory M.P. being elected for this Constituency, so take the chance to demonstrate your disapproval of the government's indifference towards Scotland's problems. To the Liberal voters I say: a vote for me is a vote for Scotland and the future. Your foremost leader, Jo Grimond, firmly believes in the need for self government. Back him up.
The aim of S.N.P. is not to win power for itself but to create a situation which allows the Scots in Scotland to rule themselves, to make their own decisions. Your choice is simple: put Scotland first or continue to vote for London rule. I hope, and believe you will vote for Scotland.
Yours for Scotland and Hamilton,
Winifred Ewing.

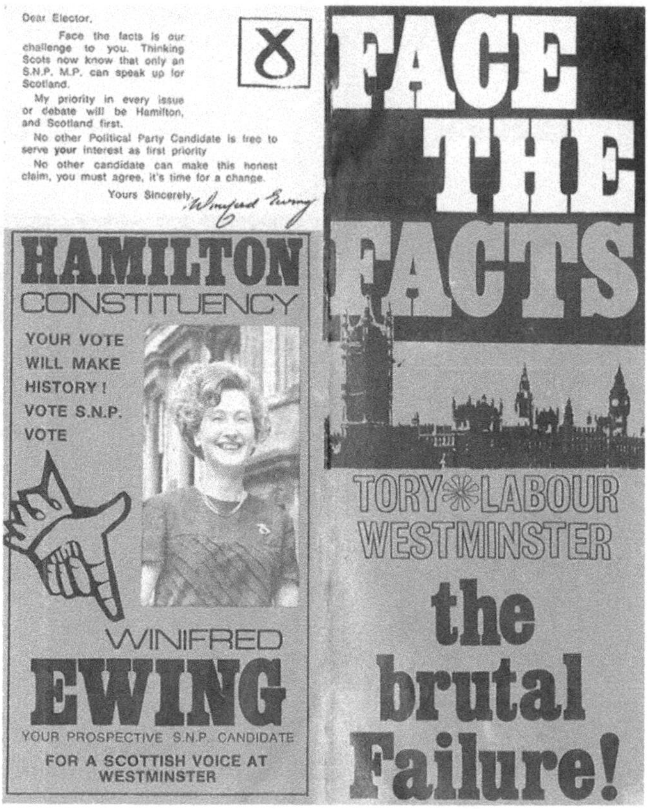
Dear Elector,
Face the facts is our challenge to you. Thinking Scots now know that only an S.N.P. M.P. can speak up for Scotland.
My priority in every issue or debate will be Hamilton, and Scotland first.
No other Political Party Candidate is free to serve your interest as first priority
No other candidate can make this honest claim, you must agree, it's time for a change.
Yours Sincerely, Winifred Ewing
FACE THE FACTS
TORY LABOUR
WESTMINSTER
the brutal Failure!
HAMILTON
CONSTITUENCY
YOUR VOTE WILL MAKE HISTORY! VOTE S.N.P. VOTE
WINIFRED
EWING
YOUR PROSPECTIVE S.N.P. CANDIDATE
FOR A SCOTTISH VOICE AT WESTMINSTER

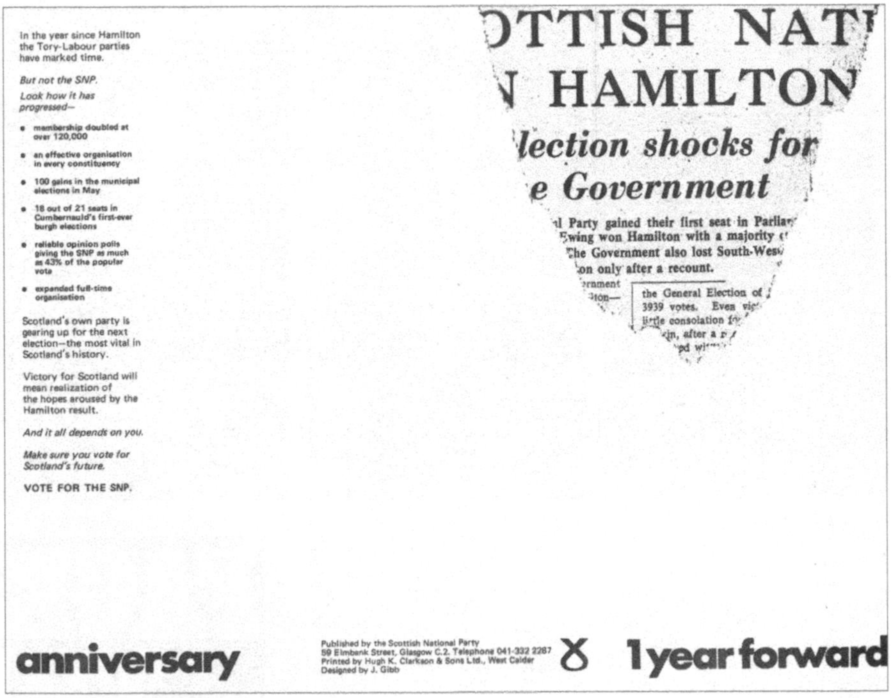

In the year since Hamilton the Tory-Labour parties have marked time.

But not the SNP.

Look how it has progressed—

- membership doubled at over 120,000
- an effective organisation in every constituency
- 100 gains in the municipal elections in May
- 18 out of 21 seats in Cumbernauld's first-ever burgh elections
- reliable opinion polls giving the SNP as much as 43% of the popular vote
- expanded full-time organisation

Scotland's own party is gearing up for the next election—the most vital in Scotland's history.

Victory for Scotland will mean realization of the hopes aroused by the Hamilton result.

And it all depends on you.

Make sure you vote for Scotland's future.

VOTE FOR THE SNP.

OTTISH NAT
N HAMILTON
lection shocks for
e Government

al Party gained their first seat in Parlia
Ewing won Hamilton with a majority
The Government also lost South-Wes
on only after a recount.

the General Election of
3939 votes. Even vi
little consolation f

anniversary

Published by the Scottish National Party
59 Elmbank Street, Glasgow C.2. Telephone 041-332 2287
Printed by Hugh K. Clarkson & Sons Ltd., West Calder
Designed by J. Gibb

1 year forward

number were active. Will Marshall, Scottish Labour's Secretary explained that 'Volunteers operate in all our constituencies but ideally it would be better to have a full-time agent in each'.[63] Labour in many parts of Scotland did not feel the need to build up a local organisation. Voters could be relied upon to turn out for the Labour candidate in sufficient numbers without any fear of losing the seat. Competition was within the party.

In July 1967, it was announced that Tom Fraser would become chair of the North of Scotland Hydro Electric Board, a member of the South of Scotland Electricity Board and the Highlands and Islands Development Board, meaning that the much anticipated by-election would go ahead. The Liberals immediately announced they would not contest the seat as there was no constituency Liberal Party. The Unionists had already adopted the 29-year-old candidate who had fought the seat at the previous year's general election. The local paper did not even refer to the SNP candidate though it had reported her speeches and activities since her adoption a year before. The focus was on Labour: 'The BIG questions NOW are when will the by-election be and who will be Labour's candidate?'[64] Neither Winnie Ewing nor Labour's Alex Wilson were mentioned in the local paper when the by-election was formally called. The expectation in Labour circles and beyond was that the battle for the Labour nomination determined who would become Hamilton's MP. There was speculation that the days when the NUM chose the candidate were over.[65] The local party fought off Will Marshall's efforts to bring in a team from Scottish headquarters, especially any interference in the selection process. Miss Sara Barker, Labour's British National Agent, had been brought in to try and calm the situation. These internal troubles created tensions that left many members disillusioned. The seat attracted considerable interest given that it was thought to offer a seat for life.

Labour had struggled to find law officers in the past. In Wilson's 1960s Government, neither the Lord Advocate nor Solicitor General had a seat in the Commons. Harry Wilson[66] was the Solicitor General at the time, having been an unsuccessful Labour candidate in the 1950s who had given up hope of a political career when he accepted the law officer's post by his friend, Scottish Secretary of State, Willie Ross. Gordon Stott had a very distinguished legal record during which he had been outspoken and independent-minded, characteristics he brought with him to the office of Lord Advocate under Harold Wilson. Aware that he was politically vulnerable, he took the opportunity to appoint himself to a seat on the Scottish bench in 1967. There were reports that Labour was anxious to have a law officer in the Commons and might impose a candidate on the constituency. Two ambitious applicants who would go on to have distinguished political careers were amongst those who sought nomination.

John McCluskey was an advocate who became Solicitor General for Scotland in 1974. As Solicitor General he led the Scottish devolution legislation in the House of Lords and proved a strong advocate of devolution. The prospect of having a lawyer of McCluskey's standing in Parliament and a potential law officer would appeal to the party's leadership and there were reports that a 'mystery lawyer' was in the running but it was known publicly who this was.[67] The other hopeful who went on to have an even more distinguished political career was John Smith. Winnie Ewing knew Smith and he was the opponent she privately most feared.[68] The local paper knew that Smith was one of the hopefuls but he was not thought to be the 'top legal name'.[69] Smith had been Labour candidate in the East Fife as a 23-year-old law student in a by-election in 1961 and stood again in East Fife, the Tories' safest Scottish seat at the time, at the 1964 general election. Smith did not stand for Parliament in 1966 but focused on his legal career, becoming an advocate in 1967. But the prospect of becoming a candidate in a safe Labour seat could not be resisted, though it was a long shot. Smith's official biographer has speculated on what might have been had Smith won the Hamilton nomination: 'it is unlikely that even he would have held the seat for

Labour, and being remembered as the man who lost Hamilton to the SNP might have killed his political career'.[70] We can never know, but Labour's defeat in Hamilton was not entirely the fault of the candidate and it is likely that neither McCluskey nor Smith could have bucked the wave of support for the SNP.

Other hopefuls included Fred Forrester, a former Coatbridge school teacher who was Assistant Secretary of Educational Institute of Scotland, and Alex Reid, who had been Tom Fraser's election agent. However, the tightest contest was between Walter Cameron, who was a popular chairman of the constituency party, and Alex Wilson, a 50-year-old High Blantyre county councillor and miners' delegate with Cooperative and trade union support.

Wilson had started work in the mines aged 14 in Wilsontown colliery, just north of the village of Forth in the neighbouring Lanark constituency, and had been an NUM official for 23 years, joining the Labour Party in 1946, as well as being a member of Lanarkshire Labour's executive. He also served as a miners' representative on Lanarkshire Advisory Committee of the Ministry of Social Security and shared past sympathies with Winnie Ewing, having previously been a supporter of the Independent Labour Party.

Cameron had no financial backer. One SNP canvasser recalls being told by voters in Blantyre well before Labour chose its candidate that, if Cameron was Labour's candidate, then Cameron would get his vote but otherwise his vote would go to the SNP.[71] There were 108 delegates at the Labour selection meeting: 48 from ward parties and 43 on union tickets, including 18 from the NUM, and 17 Cooperative movement delegates. Some subsequent reports, following Labour's defeat, suggest that the NUM dominated the local Labour Party but the NUM constituted only about 16 per cent of delegates. There were no longer any operational mines in the constituency.[72]

However, what the NUM could offer was financial support.

Wilson followed Duncan Graham and Tom Fraser as the third successive miner to stand for Labour in the seat since 1918. According to Tam Dalyell, the Scottish Area Executive of the National Union of Mineworkers (NUM) met shortly after Fraser's resignation and ensured that two local NUM miners were blocked and the union supported Wilson. Dalyell placed emphasis on the role of Mick McGahey and brothers Abe and Alex Moffat, the leading Communist Party NUM officials, in deciding 'who should inherit "their" coal-miners' parliamentary seat', favouring Wilson, who was 'supposedly a "fellow traveller"'.[73] There was resentment and some Labour activists were reportedly unwilling to help, no doubt assuming that Labour would hold the seat in any case.

Wilson was a miner in Polkemmet in West Lothian.[74] Being from the 'other side of the Clyde' with council experience that 'looked towards Lanark' rather than Hamilton meant that he was without local allegiances or allies, and it was this that was thought to have undermined him.[75] Labour members seemed to have been annoyed by the idea of having a candidate who lived on the border of the constituency, even though neither of the other candidates lived in the county at all. Dalyell refers to a widely held belief that Wilson was a Catholic in a constituency that included 'Lesmahagow and Larkhall, towns which were the epicentre of the Orange Order in Scotland'. Sectarian politics were never far below the surface in internal Labour politics in Lanarkshire.

Many people blamed the Labour candidate for the defeat but at the time of his selection the local paper described him as a 'formidable character' with a reputation as a 'bonny fechter', and, like his namesake at No.10, was 'articulate and expert in dealing with hecklers';[76] though it also questioned whether the 'traditional mining socialism which he represents is geared to a constituency that has changed in the last few years – "semi-detacheds instead of miners' rows"'.[77]

Subsequent commentaries have tended to portray Wilson as an extremely poor candidate, but such accounts need to be treated with care as a number also include basic factual errors and fail to take account of the limited time Wilson had to establish himself in the constituency. One interpretation offered by a political scientist at the time was scathing of Labour's attitude: 'the local Labour leaders behaved as though Hamilton were a snug and safe Labour bailiwick... they chose a pleasant local party stalwart... They apparently did not stop to consider that he might prove to be a dumb dog at press conferences and on television.'[78] Wilson returned as Hamilton's MP in 1970 and his eight year Parliamentary record hardly conforms with any notion of him being a 'fellow traveller'. What was far more significant was his attitude, shared by many in his party, that the seat belonged to Labour. Retrospective explanations sit uneasily with contemporary expectations. Labour was a 6–1 bet according to the bookies at the time that Alex Wilson won the Labour nomination.[79] Wilson himself was unknown to the journalists, or at least those journalists from outside the constituency, who were waiting outside the hall for the results of the decision.[80]

Local campaigning

In the 1960s, the conventional wisdom was that election outcomes were determined by national campaigns. Research conducted by two political scientists in Dundee challenged this view and showed that local campaigning could make a significant difference.[81] Conventional wisdom today is that local campaigning can make a difference.[82] That is more likely to be the case in a by-election. The Hamilton writ was moved on 12 October 1967 and the by-election was held on 2 November making it formally a very short campaign but the SNP had been active in the constituency for over a year. The party was confident it could do better than it had in Pollok. By this stage, it had about 1,000 members in Hamilton and four branches, whereas there were only 200 members in Pollok when the campaign there had been launched.

Arthur Donaldson, SNP leader, set out the task before his party: 'the many thousands who are completely disillusioned with the Labour

Party must be persuaded to vote SNP; the Tories of the last election must be shown that the vote which will count this time will be for the SNP; we must persuade the Did-Not-Votes to come out this time for the SNP (they have something at last to vote for); we must fight any suggestions towards abstension; and we must know where our support is and organise to get it out solidly on polling day'.[83] There was little evidence of sophisticated targeting of voters. The party did not have enough information on who was most likely to vote for it and there was a strong tendency in the party leadership to assume that all voters were equally amenable to the SNP's message. As they saw it, the SNP was a *national* party and should avoid appearing to act in the interests of any sectoral interest.

The SNP was convinced that the effort put into a by-election campaign could pay off. But it was not an entirely smooth campaign. In 1966, the party created what it called a Mobile Information Service (MIS). This sounded much grander than it was, as became clear during the by-election. The MIS was a van with a faulty gear box with, as Ewing reported to the party's national executive committee in mid-August, a 'deteriorating appearance' and which had to eventually be withdrawn from service.[84] One of the party's vice chairs was given the task of checking out whether the van could be repaired and gave Arthur Donaldson authority to authorise spending to provide a van for the by-election.

Each week SNP HQ sent missives to branches urging members to help. This became another common feature of SNP by-elections, with activists from the length and breadth of Scotland travelling to Hamilton. A prize was awarded to Glasgow Shettleston branch as the one which had given most person-hours to the campaign. A newsletter sent to members in August 1967 informed them that the campaign was proceeding apace and that the first canvass was 'well underway' and that the first leaflet was being distributed. There was a call for more help in order to complete the distribution of the leaflet and canvass by the end of September.[85] Concern was expressed about the lack of urgency in the *Scots Independent*, in an article entitled 'Scotland Free by Seventy Three', two months before the by-election. The weekly *Scots Independent* carried details for those intending to help out and encouraged members to make contact in advance of coming to Hamilton to 'avoid frustration and wasted effort for all concerned'.[86] There was a fear that members thought there was still plenty of time as the date for the by-election had not yet been set.[87] Ewing urged members attending the party's National Council to put in an effort, 'If we get 60 people from outside the constituency every week night from now on, in addition to all our local workers, then we are set to win.'[88]

The SNP organised 'car cavalcades', streams of cars plastered with Ewing and SNP posters with a number of loudspeakers blaring out taped music and messages from the candidate. The impression sought was of a party with momentum. Public meetings were held throughout the constituency. An indication of the relative interest in these meetings was provided in a report of Labour and SNP public meetings in Quarter, a small ex-mining village in the constituency. The chair of the Labour meeting introduced Wilson as 'eminently suited' as he was a miner 'like most of you'. It attracted an audience of 20, including four Nationalists with the rest over 50 years of age. The following evening, Ewing attracted 80, mostly under 40.[89] Ewing spoke about Scotland joining the rest of the world, 'At the UNO we'd sit between Saudi Arabia and Senegal. I *want* to be an internationalist, I *want* us to be at all those tables: we have a lot to offer.'[90] The SNP could hardly have chosen a better advocate of this internationalist nationalism than Winnie Ewing.

The comment most frequently made by those involved in the SNP campaign is that it was fun – they took politics seriously but made sure it was enjoyable. Leafleting and canvassing was followed by less conventional engagement with the public. Blantyre branch ran a 'Miss SNP Dance' in March attended by minor celebrities. Cliff Hanley, writer and journalist, and Ian Cuthbertson, actor and then art director of Glasgow's Citizens' Theatre, and a couple of local doctors judged the competition. Someone who knew Ewing later and had spoken to her about the by-election refers to Ewing's 'campaigning by shopping', referring to her breezy style of engaging with people going about their everyday business. She was prepared to engage in stunts – photographed with a monkey on her shoulder and on top of the globe at the David Livingstone Fountain at Blantyre. Ewing's view was that believing that Hamilton could be won was important to victory. The key moment for all activists was when they believed that the SNP could win. The campaign's self-belief reflected the self-confidence that Ewing felt was required for self-government.

At the start of his campaign, Alex Wilson said he was convinced those who had voted SNP in the local elections would support him and that he would not be concentrating on any major local issues, but would rely on support from people happy with his party's past achievements. The message was unusual given the difficulties faced by Harold Wilson's Government and evidence that the local Labour council was relatively popular. His examples drew on matters close to him. The Government and Hamilton Council had done a 'magnificent job in changing the face of what was once a mining area'. The one remaining coal bing in Hamilton would be removed with an 80 per cent grant for the council from the Government and he claimed that other problems had been solved by increased rating relief and extra grants for house building and road improvements.[91]

Labour tended to dismiss the SNP contemptuously as an irrelevant irritant. Willie Ross, with characteristic scorn, referred to the SNP as the 'Scottish Nark Party'. Ewing embraced the abuse by responding that she intended to 'go on narking'.[92] The *Hamilton Advertiser*'s chief reporter would later describe Willie Ross hating the SNP 'with a passion bordering on xenophobia'.[93] Ewing promised to become the most expensive MP by asking lots of questions in Parliament. Ross continued with the 'Nark' comment at a stormy public meeting a week before polling day which heard interruptions and heckling due to the SNP supporters in attendance. He insisted that the SNP were ignorant and should learn more about what the Government was doing for Scotland and argued that only a UK Government could prevent the uncontrolled drift of industry southwards, bringing industry to Scotland from the south and Midlands.[94]

Gregor Mackenzie, MP for neighbouring Rutherglen, had been instructed to make a series of speeches in Hamilton on the Government's economic, financial and particularly taxation policies. He sought help from Harold Lever, Treasury Minister: 'Since we are being opposed by the Scottish Nationalist Party I will be under an obligation to refer to the Scottish position.'[95] Treasury support was enlisted to refute SNP claims in a leaflet being distributed in the constituency. The Treasury response he received was not as helpful as he had wanted: '...precise figures of the taxation and expenditure attributable to Scotland cannot be achieved just because Scotland is not a separate country and there is no record of transactions passing over the Border'.[96] But Mackenzie was unusual in focusing on the SNP. Until the closing stages of the by-election, Labour had tried to ignore the Nationalist threat.

Iain Dyer, Tory candidate, referred to the generational changes that were happening, conveying the sense that Labour's support was draining away and that it was becoming a party of old men. It is impossible to test the extent to which this feeling existed but it was a startling claim coming so soon after the mood of optimism and modernisation. It is understandable if there was a sense of the passing of a generation of substantial Labour figures. Clement Attlee, Labour's post-war leader, died in early October. And locally, Labour lost Bob Smillie, one of its best known local trade union supporters.[97] A week before polling day, the Labour Provost of Hamilton also died, removing Labour's one seat overall majority on the council. There was a sense that an era was ending for Labour.

Expectations shattered

The *Sunday Mail* published the results of a 'straw poll' in one council housing estate four days before polling day which found that 18 electors would vote SNP, five Labour, one Tory and six were Don't Knows or would not vote.[98] The *Sunday Post* reported a 'very significant swing away from Labour which is going to the Scottish Nationalists rather than the Tories'.[99] The *Daily Record* published the results of another poll, again conducted in a rather unscientific manner, two days before the vote which was headlined, 'Labour is far from home in Hamilton'.[100] It suggested that 46 per cent would vote SNP, the actual proportion of the SNP vote, allowing it to win the seat. It underestimated Labour support and over stated the Tories but the headline message ought to have rung alarm bells in Labour rooms.

The final editorial in the *Hamilton Advertiser* before polling day suggested that the result was a 'foregone conclusion' and that it was 'hard to believe that there can be other than a Labour victory' but if proved wrong, suggested that the 'other Mr Wilson should take a long rest from politics'. The world-weary editorial complained that the world of politics was 'dull and dingy' and that Britain had 'lost its vocation, its sense of destiny as a nation' and repeated former American Secretary of State Dean Acheson's comment five years before that Britain had lost an Empire but yet to find a role. The SNP was dismissed for its 'small minded parochialism', the Socialists were a 'pathetic irrelevance' and the Conservatives stood for a 'world of the day before yesterday'.[101]

The three candidates were given a last chance to offer their programmes to the electorate in the local paper. Iain Dyer claimed Tory credit for the for the M74 motorway, legislation leading to the removal of the coal bings and new factories in Scotland. He noted that spending per head of population in Scotland on housing, schools and industrial development was higher than south of the border.

Alex Wilson started by emphasising that unemployment was too high, blamed Scottish industrialists who were 'less enterprising than their English brothers' and listed measures taken by the Labour Government to improve investment. He too took a pot shot at the SNP, suggesting that building a 'wall from the Solway to the Tweed' would not help. He repeated the line Ross had made during the campaign that industries had been directed to the area from England by the Wilson Government, suggesting that it was important to refuse permission for industrial expansion in London and the Midlands to assist places like Lanarkshire. The thrust of the argument from both Labour and the Tories was anti-SNP, suggesting where they saw the threat coming from by the end of the campaign. Ewing noted that Labour had held Hamilton since the constituency was created in 1918 during which time one million Scots had emigrated. She ran through a list of grievances against the Labour Government and argued for a voice at Westminster for Scotland 'without fear or favour'.[102]

The *Glasgow Herald*'s reflections on the day of the by-election suggested that what was expected to have been a dull affair compared with the marginal Pollok by-election but proved more interesting largely because of the SNP *joie de vivre*, employing 'modern marketing techniques and audio-visual aids'.[103] The SNP had reworked folk songs to give them explicitly nationalist messages. The Tories joined in with their own campaign song towards the end of the campaign, gaining media attention by noting that it had been written by a local Tory activist who shared the same name as the Labour Prime Minister's wife, Mary Wilson.

With only five days to go, Alex Wilson took the day off saying, 'You can say it is 90 per cent confidence and 10 per cent need.'[104] The *Observer* reported on Labour's disbelief that there was any danger, quoting an insider, 'We didn't count the votes here, we weighed them.'[105] Labour's candidate was described in the press as almost invisible. Less than a month before polling day, a columnist for the local paper suggested that the red flag was 'kept so high that one can't see it' and asked if anyone had seen Alex Wilson apart from the party faithful.[106] This was unfair as Labour's campaign was only officially launched on 12 October – three weeks after choosing the candidate and less than three weeks before polling day. The fault was less the candidate's than the arty leadership's. Labour's official launch in Larkhall saw Wilson sharing a platform with Secretary of State Willie Ross and James Jack, general secretary of the Scottish Trades Union Congress (STUC), who was originally from Blantyre. As the party was confident of winning, it made sense to have a low key campaign and avoid any slips. The problem was misplaced confidence and a failure to appreciate that the SNP had been fighting a campaign for over a year. It was a view reinforced by the media. In its last issue before the election, the *Hamilton Advertiser* thought the SNP might just replace the Tories for second place but expected Labour would have a majority of at least 5,000.[107] On polling day, the *Scotsman* predicted that Labour would win 17,000 votes, SNP 12,000 and the Tories 10,000. The bookies, usually reliable guides, were all clear. Labour was set to win.

By-election issues

There were a number of issues that came up in the by-election. A key lesson learned particularly in West Lothian, was that actively campaigning on local issues could pay dividends. Local knowledge and the lengthy campaign allowed Winnie Ewing to become familiar with matters that directly worried constituents. This was a period when abortion and capital punishment regularly featured in campaigns but there was little difference between the candidates and no candidate was keen to make these election issues. Winnie Ewing outlined a series of policy positions. She supported comprehensive education at a parents' association meeting, arguing that this 'avoided labelling 70 per cent of the children as failures at the age of 11 or 12'.[108] At one public meeting during the by-election she had noted that net emigration in 1964 had been 40,000 and had risen to 43,000 in 1965 which was 'like losing the whole population of Hamilton each year, and this helps disguise the unemployment figures'. She criticised the Government's Selective Employment Tax (SET), designed to help manufacturing industries from proceeds from service industries and help exports, suggesting it was 'extremely irresponsible to apply it to Scotland'.[109] SET had perverse effects and was deeply unpopular hitting service industries hard without the advantages hoped for.[110]

The Vietnam War was raging. Iain Dyer was shocked to be asked his views on the Vietnam War and thought that Scotland was going through a 'revolution'.[111] In late October, Richard Crossman recorded his view that the Vietnam war was becoming 'more and more a great moral issue' and that the Labour Government would find it 'more and more difficult to keep to their policy of remaining America's staunch and loyal ally' against the 'growing moral protest of their own rank and file'.[112] Massive demonstrations against the war took place in America and across the world, including one in Glasgow two weekends before the by-election. The UK had been under pressure from the USA to commit troops to Vietnam but Harold Wilson had refused. The Labour leadership was defeated at its annual conference in Scarborough in early October on a resolution on Vietnam which called on the Government to 'dissociate themselves completely from the United States'. A delegate from Inverness spoke in favour of the resolution while Foreign Secretary George Brown, recently back from meeting Lyndon Johnson, spoke against.[113] Winnie Ewing was unambiguously critical of American policy in Vietnam. Alex Wilson was reported to be against American bombing of North Vietnam, the only issue on which he adopted a position critical of the Labour Government.[114]

Ewing's position was similar to Labour's conference policy though the SNP was officially more ambivalent, adopting a position not dissimilar to the Labour Government. The SNP had campaigned against nuclear weapons on the Clyde and there had been protests against the siting of nuclear weapons in Scottish bases. Once more, Ewing was in tune with a mood prevalent across the left in Scotland at the time. While most voters in Hamilton may not have changed their vote on Vietnam or nuclear weapons, her stance likely contributed to her image as a progressive political figure. Though it was not a major issue on the doorsteps, membership of the EEC was a matter Winnie Ewing was keen to address. Her views on Europe were shaped by personal experiences and her understanding of the role of small states. Two key elements of her Europeanism were evident during the by-election. She understood the way small states were heard in the EEC and referred to Luxembourg, with half a million people having a voice in the negotiations over the UK's application to join the EEC. In March 1967, she called for Scotland to have voting representatives in negotiations.[115] In a speech six months later, she insisted that the Scottish legal system would 'fit in very well if ever we entered the Common Market'.[116] This view had been articulated by Lord Kilbrandon in a speech a year before. Court of Session judge Kilbrandon, who would later chair the Royal Commission on the Constitution which reported in 1973, spoke at an event celebrating the 1320 Arbroath Declaration, suggested that it might be necessary to make another 'declaration of independence within an international community'. As a judge, he offered no view on membership of the EEC but maintained that an urgent question of constitutional law arose, 'If Britain were to join the Six, it will become not seven but eight' and it would be appropriate for Scotland to play a part in the EEC as a nation and people.[117]

Ewing repeatedly expressed her support for independence in an internationalist context. When she addressed the annual Bannockburn rally in July 1967, she insisted that Scotland was part of Europe and 'not isolationist in international affairs but a participant in all that nationhood demanded' and argued that Scots shared a 'tradition of learning and of legal thought with Europe'.[118] During the by-election she announced that she had written to De Gaulle 'dissociating Scotland from the UK's application to join the common market'.[119] Twelve years later, on becoming a directly elected Member of the European Parliament, she would join the European Progressive Democrats which included French Gaullists and Fianna Fail. Commentators from London who covered the by-election, and were new to the SNP, were surprised at the SNP's message. This was not nationalism as they had conventionally understood it. The author of a half-page article in the *Observer* following the election seemed surprised to find that the SNP was 'anti-London, in the sense of being anti-centre and anti-Establishment' but 'they are not all anti-England'. They wanted to negotiate Scotland's own entry into the EEC, 'Fervent nationalists, they are no less dedicated internationalists.'[120]

The Tories

The Tories had already chosen Iain Dyer, a lawyer living in Bearsden, as candidate. Dyer had been the Unionist Party candidate at the previous year's general election and he would go on to become a Glasgow City Councillor. The Tories focused on the SNP. Edward Heath, party leader, launched the Tory campaign in early September. In an indication of the issues that commonly came up in elections at this time, Heath was asked to sign a petition by a local Tory activist demanding the restoration of the death penalty which he refused to do.[121] The absence of a hanger-and-flogger on the ballot paper ensured capital punishment was not a major issue in the election.

Heath dismissed the SNP threat as 'ten per cent passionate and 80 per cent protest vote'.[122] A fortnight after launching their Hamilton campaign, the Tories took Walthamstow West from Labour on a swing of just over 18 per cent. Hamilton would require a 21 per cent swing and Sir Gilmour Menzies Anderson, chair of the party in Scotland, maintained that this was possible given that north east London was hardly affected by unemployment compared with Hamilton and there would be momentum following the Pollok result in March.[123]

But behind the scenes the Tories were worried. Conservative Central Office conducted research including polls for each by-election. This would be shared with the constituency agents. The report on Hamilton prepared in July noted that the 'tide of nationalism is running strongly in Hamilton' and there was a 'danger that we might do very badly'. The SNP was 'taking very heavily from Scottish Conservatives'. Headquarters in London insisted that it was 'clearly vital, armed with this advance information, that Scotland should organise its Hamilton campaign with a view to minimising the Nationalist threat.'[124] A private survey for the Tories of 200 Hamilton voters in mid-September found that general economic problems and housing were top of the list of concerns. Unemployment was a cause of concern, a subject that the party had not found in by-election surveys since the previous winter. Sixty-five per cent of the electorate expected to be affected by the economic situation, a higher proportion than in any previous by-election surveys, with the cost of living being most frequently mentioned but unemployment of great significance. Ewing had already picked this up on the doorsteps.

People, especially women, were worried about rising prices and the cost of living. It did not help when reports appeared in the media in the weeks leading up to the by-election that gas prices were set to rise.[125] The survey also detected a disaffection with the two main parties with 42 per cent thinking it would be a good thing if the SNP did well. This feeling was more pronounced amongst Conservative than Labour supporters. People were much more satisfied with the local council and education than had been the case in Pollok. This was important given that there was a higher proportion of council housing in Hamilton compared with Pollok. Labour was viewed by most voters as caring most about the problems of the area. The survey also confirmed what academic research was finding. Almost all Catholics expressed support for Labour.[126]

A series of high profile Tories spoke at public meetings in support of Dyer: Esmond Wright, recently returned MP for Pollok, was followed by Shadow Chancellor of the Exchequer Iain MacLeod, former Prime Minister Sir Alec Douglas-Home, former Scottish Secretary Michael Noble, George Younger, Ayr's MP and future Cabinet Minister, Norman Wylie, Edinburgh Pentlands MP and past and future Scottish law officer and Perth MP Ian MacArthur. While Ewing could call upon senior SNP figures, none could compete with the public profile of her opponents' supporting speakers, until she had the support of someone outside her party.

Celebrities and troops

Magnus Magnusson described 'Scotnattery', the various splinter groups of the Scottish national movement, in a tongue-in-cheek article in 1961. In the closing week of the by-election, he admitted that he 'never dreamed in six short years Scottish Nationalism could have hauled itself out of the welter of petty disputes into its present position'.[127] He maintained that 'everybody – and I use that term very loosely – wants the Nationalists to win'. What he meant was that there was widespread support amongst Scottish journalists for an SNP victory. This was not a commitment to self-government but a desire for more excitement in what was seen as the stale world of Scottish politics. Magnusson believed that having a Nationalist MP would 'help to spark debate' on Scotland's future. He admitted that it might be impertinent for an Icelandic citizen to offer an opinion but he wanted the SNP to win as he hoped it would shock Labour and the Tories into 'harder thinking by failure, and the SNP shocked into clearer thinking by success.'[128]

Another public figure entered the debate in the final week of the campaign. On 11 September, Ewing received a 'surprising offer' from Ludovic Kennedy offering to speak for her at the by-election. Kennedy was a well-known broadcaster and Liberal Party member. He stood for the Liberals in the 1958 Rochdale by-election, coming second with 35 per cent of the vote in what had been a tight

Labour-Conservative marginal at the previous general election. He managed the Liberals' television strategy in the 1966 election and the broadcast that he produced was deemed to be one of the 'most effective of election broadcasts'.[129]

Ewing understood that Kennedy was about to leave the Liberals but had not yet done so. She and others in Hamilton were keen on Kennedy's support but sought SNP leader Arthur Donaldson's view.[130] Donaldson urged caution and thought Kennedy's offer gave Ewing problems. He worried that she might lose votes if Kennedy was still a Liberal and that she should find out what he was intending to say in advance but if Kennedy left the Liberals and explained why then this would help and even more so if he joined the SNP. Donaldson thought that Ewing should 'play this one from strength'. It was a remarkable attitude. There was the leader of a party without any Parliamentary representation playing hard to get with a distinguished television personality who had previously stood for Parliament for the Liberals, a party that increased its seats from nine to twelve at the previous year's election. In the event, Kennedy informed his local Liberal Constituency Association – David Steel's Roxburgh, Selkirk and Peebles – of his resignation but decided not to join the SNP, making it easy for Ewing to accept his offer.[131] Two days before the by-election he attended a meeting of Edinburgh University Nationalist club and on the eve of poll shared a platform with Winnie Ewing and Jimmy Halliday, former SNP leader, in Hamilton. A sense of momentum was being created in the national media underscored by the level of SNP activism in Hamilton. There were other endorsements. World Boxing champion Walter McGowan, who was from Hamilton, lent his support. Sean Connery, by then having starred in five James Bond films, gave public support to the SNP with a signed leaflet including a photograph of Connery, as he had done in Pollok. Minor celebrities offered support as did many people with specialist media skills.

SNP activists from across Scotland poured into Hamilton during the by-election. Illustrative of this commitment was the young recently married couple from Arbroath referred to in the introduction.[132] There were 29 polling stations in the Hamilton constituency including one in Rosebank with 158 electors. The SNP was keen to have members outside each polling station throughout the day and this required many activists as well as activists needed to get out the vote. SNP supporters came into the constituency from various parts of Scotland as well as supporters from Wales on polling day.

The party's balance sheet for 1967 gives an indication of the effort that was put into the by-election. It had been a long campaign which started well before the by-election had officially been called. Angus MacGillveray's Alba Pools had brought in over £8,000, constituting over 80 per cent of its income at the end of 1967.[133] The accounts included an item headed 'Parliamentary Research and By-Election expenses' amounting to £2,677 (equivalent of £45,800 in 2017), over a quarter of the party's national income. Towards the end of the campaign, the Tories accused the SNP of over-spending and suggested that if Ewing won she would be debarred from taking up her seat.[134] But the total expenditure was spread across many months before the official campaign began and included post-election support. Iain Dyer was quick to distance himself from the accusations realising that this was close to an admission that the SNP were the real contenders against Labour. But the main resource was the energy of the party's activists.

Polling day, the count and the result

The local paper's first edition on Friday 3 November was printed too early to catch the result but the decision had been taken to produce an unprecedented later edition that would carry the result. The early edition suggested that the inclement weather might help the SNP because their supporters were the 'most fervid and unlikely to be deterred by the cold wind and rain' but stuck to the view that Labour would hold the seat. It would 'take an awful lot of steam to dampen down Labour's 16,576 majority of last year'. It suggested that Ewing's campaign set a 'cracking pace' at the outset – it had been 'flamboyant, exuberant, intense' – but she had lost her 'super ring of confidence and replaced it with "quiet confidence"' at the end. Blantyre and Larkhall were thought to be the SNP's best areas. We can only speculate on the extent to which Ewing attracted Orange voters disillusioned with the Tories in places like Larkhall. There was no conscious effort to appeal to the Orange vote but that did not mean that this vote was not attracted to the Ewing. She herself would speculate many years later that having a second cousin who had played for Glasgow Rangers might have contributed to the belief that she had connections with Larkhall's large Rangers supporting population.[135]

Labour was prepared to admit to a drop in its majority but not below 8,000. The Labour campaign had been the 'most sober, workmanlike rather than spectacular'.[136] In normal circumstances as the incumbent sitting on a very large majority that might have seemed like a sensible approach but unknown to Labour or the *Hamilton Advertiser* this was an unusual by-election. The *Advertiser* judged Iain Dyer to have lasted the pace and performed on television best. The *Advertiser* damned all of the candidates in equal measure. While the editorial a week before bemoaned the 'dull and dingy' campaign, this article moaned complained that personalities were becoming too important but judged that on this basis Ewing would be drinking champagne in the morning. She was the 'darling of the press'. 'Winnie the Woo', as one columnist called the SNP candidate, was described as charming and winsome by journalists who 'wanted her to win. What a story!'. There was more than a little truth in this.[137]

For the first time in the *Hamilton Advertiser*'s 111 year history, half the print run of the paper was delayed to allow the final result to be available in Hamilton with the early edition sent to places outside the constituency. A very different headline was needed:

'Winnie Wins by a Mile!' 'Labour were stunned. The Tories were humiliated.'[138] Three decades later, George Downie, who had been the *Advertiser*'s chief reporter in 1967, concluded that the headline was a 'massive understatement'.[139] Winifred Ewing was forever after Winnie. The original plan had been to replace a report on Labour's victory with a more detailed account but within an hour of the polls closing it was clear to the paper's journalists that something dramatic was about to happen. Its chief reporter returned to the paper's office to prepare a report, assuming that Winnie Ewing had won. Each candidate had been interviewed with answers from each for different scenarios but these were abandoned as they were 'too staid' given the emerging result and the need for immediate reaction to a sensational result. A 17-year-old was readied to take these responses back to the chief reporter as this was thought more reliable than phoning the comments into the paper. The picture of Winnie Ewing on the front page – a windswept Ewing in front of Lanarkshire County Buildings – had to be drawn from an SNP leaflet such was the paper's lack of preparedness for the result. The paper's early editions carried stories about a Lanark factory immunising workers against flu and tenants protesting at the County Buildings but these were removed to provide more coverage of the result in the second edition.[140]

Tom Fraser refused to comment when the *Hamilton Advertiser* called him at 12.25am after the declaration. The *Advertiser* was clear that the by-election had been lost in London. On the platform after the declaration, Ewing thanked voters for 'making history'. The version of her speech reported in the local paper quoted her saying, 'We are climbing back on to the map again. We have an independent voice in Westminster.'[141] It has subsequently been retold as 'Stop the world, Scotland wants to get on' and many present insist this was indeed what was said SNP activists joined the candidate after the declaration in the Zambezi Hotel, where the activists had often gathered throughout the campaign. The *Hamilton Advertiser* ensured that copies of the second edition of the paper were delivered to the hotel.

Conclusion

There was nothing inevitable about the SNP victory in Hamilton. It is impossible to know what might have happened if one or many different choices had been made: if the by-election had been caused for some reason other than providing Tom Fraser with a well-paid public office; if Labour had adopted another candidate; and if it had been a longer campaign. But the wider context in which the shine had come off the Harold Wilson's Labour Government – facing major economic and industrial relations challenges – was important. But even the combination of matters within and outside Labour's control do not alone explain the outcome. The SNP's candidate and campaign were a perfect match for these turbulent political times.

CHAPTER THREE

The Fallout

> Politics in Scotland since 1966 has been dominated by the flow and ebb of Scottish nationalism.[1]

> We decided years ago that 'going it alone' was the only way to secure freedom. Our experience of alliances, arrangements, compromises, and acts during the years before the present 'hard line' of Nationalist politics was evolved had proved finally that no friends unwilling to put Scotland first, and to abandon loyalties other than Scottish loyalties, were to be trusted when the political battle was joined.[2]

> The technological revolution was light years away from Hamilton's weary committee rooms where well-meaning ladies prepared mountains of food and gallons of tea for election workers who never came.[3]

> The election of Mrs Ewing has galvanised the Scottish MPs into asking a flood of questions.[4]

Introduction

SIR ALEC CAIRNCROSS noted that the 'crisis moves nearer' in his diary a week after the by-election.[5] He was referring to the economic crisis, with poor trade figures about to be published which would put pressure on the exchange rate. The pound was devalued just over a fortnight after the by-election. But there was also a political crisis following the Hamilton by-election. Less than three weeks after the by-election, an opinion poll put the SNP on 37 per cent of the vote in Scotland, double that of the Conservatives, and only three points behind Labour.[6] Cairncross speculated that a very high proportion of young people supported the SNP as he was sure that older voters were not so impressed by the nationalists. The sense of a new assertive generation emerging in the context of economically difficult times would concentrate minds in Westminster and Whitehall. This was not what the Government's chief economic adviser had envisioned at the start of the year.

The general view in Scotland was that the by-election was not a flash event. The Church and Nation Committee of the Church of Scotland, a particularly influential body at this time, offered its 'deliverance' (or opinion) on the by-election. It took the view that this was 'not a passing phenomenon which can be alleviated by minor measures of further devolution or dispelled by an improvement in economic conditions. The growing concern for recognition of Scotland's nationhood and for greater control by Scots over their national affairs arises from causes which cannot be so easily remedied or removed.'[7]

The Times predicted a low turnout as 'former Labour dependables voting with their carpet slippers' would simply stay at home. It doubted turnout would be over 70 per cent.[8] In fact, turnout in Hamilton was slightly up on the previous year's general election and on an electoral register that was 13 months old. The Tory vote collapsed and it is fair to assume that much of this anti-Labour vote moved to the SNP, but Labour's vote fell even further than expected. When 30 per cent of Labour's vote in the previous year's election disappeared it was impossible to spin the result as the SNP winning on the back of Tory votes.

Two other by-elections were being defended by Labour on the same day as Hamilton. Of the three, South West Leicester was thought to be the most vulnerable, requiring a nine per cent swing to the Conservatives. The bookies thought the Leicester seat was the most likely to see a Labour defeat. The Conservatives won the seat with just over half the vote. But Labour held on in Manchester Gorton with a majority of 557 against Winston Churchill, grandson of former Prime Minister, standing for the Conservatives. But it was Hamilton that captured most attention.

Candidate	Party	Votes	%	+/-
Iain Dyer	Conservative and Unionist Party	4,986	12.5	– 16.4
Winifred Ewing	Scottish National Party	18,397	46.0	46.0
Alexander Wilson	Labour	16,598	41.5	– 29.7
	Majority	1,779	4.5	
	Turnout	39,981	73.7	

Taking up her seat

After such a demanding schedule, Winnie Ewing took a few days off on a family holiday to Shetland for which she was criticised by a couple of Scottish Labour MPs. Willie Hamilton would become one of Ewing's, and the SNP's, most bitter critics in the years ahead. Her short holiday allowed the party to arrange her Commons entrance. A special train was chartered, the 'Tartan Express'. The train travelled overnight via Edinburgh, where it stopped to pick up SNP President Robert McIntyre and others. By all accounts, it was an all-night party for many on the train and arrived in London at 7am where it was met by a crowd who had already arrived or drawn from SNP supporters in London and surrounding area. Pipers had sent them off from Glasgow and welcomed them in London. Three Minis awaited the Ewing family and others close to the campaign to take them from King's Cross station to their hotel. Ewing would later address a meeting in Caxton Hall, only ten minutes from the Commons, consisting of Welsh and Scottish Nationalists, a kind of dress rehearsal for entering the Commons.

Lord Boyd-Orr, founder of the Rowett Research Institute and Director General of the UN Food and Agriculture Organisation, was amongst those watching Ewing take up her seat. Boyd Orr was elected as Independent MP for the Scottish Universities the day after Robert McIntyre won the Motherwell by-election for the SNP in 1945. In his victory speech, McIntyre had expressed hope that he would be joined by Boyd-Orr given the latter's strong support for self-government. Boyd-Orr was essentially the second Scottish Nationalist to be elected to the Commons, though as an Independent. He was keen to be in the Peers' Gallery to watch Winnie Ewing take up her seat while McIntyre sat in the public gallery. Boyd-Orr waved to Ewing, acknowledging her success and continuation of a campaign which he had long supported.[9] Whereas McIntyre had initially refused to take sponsors, Ewing was sponsored by Gwynfor Evans and Alasdair Mackenzie, Liberal MP for Ross and Cromarty.

The media and the SNP

There was a symbiotic relationship between the SNP and the media. In an article a few days before the by-election, the journalist Magnus Magnusson maintained that the Nationalist challenge made 'good copy' and an SNP victory would 'enliven the political scene no end' and therefore the press 'play it up no end'.[10] James Kellas believed that the press, particularly the *Express* and *Scotsman*, had 'fanned the flame.'[11] The SNP's now familiar symbol, drawing inspiration from Gerald Holtom's symbol designed for the Campaign for Nuclear Disarmament, combining a thistle and the Scottish saltire, had been used in Billy Wolfe's by-election campaign and was used in all subsequent elections. The party was beginning to look more professional. The SNP produced the *Hamilton Herald*, a mocked up local newspaper complete with local news and horoscopes.

The BBC started 'Debate', a weekly political programme in autumn 1967. The *Radio Times* described the new programme as a direct response to the rise of the SNP in local elections and the Pollok by-election. Ewing was offered columns in the *Daily Record* and the *Scottish Daily Express*, opting for the former as its more working class Labour supporting readership would be a key target for the party. The *Express* carried a weekly 'Winnie at Westminster' column, following her activities as a prism on Scottish politics in London. Ewing felt that she could not write in the style required and her weekly column was ghosted by *Record* journalist Michael Grieve. Grieve would meet Ewing each week to discuss the column. Harry Gourlay, Labour MP for Kirkcaldy, accused Ewing of being a 'well paid tool of the *Daily Record* and *Daily Express* who are competing with each other to cash in on the present upsurge of nationalism'.[12] The *Express* rejected the suggestion pointing out that Ewing was not paid for the weekly coverage but there was little doubt that the papers competed to cover a subject for which there was ample public interest. Alistair Dunnett, editor of the *Scotsman*, began to take home rule seriously after Hamilton. He would devote considerable effort to examining the question and the paper became a leading advocate of home rule.[13] In February 1968, *The Scotsman* published a series of article on how Scotland should be governed which were later produced as a booklet.[14] Home rule was firmly on the agenda of key sections of the media.

Gordon Wilson reported that Ewing had answered 2000 letters, made 33 radio or television broadcasts and given 400 press interviews as well as speaking in the Commons, asking 61 Parliamentary Questions in her first month as an MP.[15] In her first year as an MP, she reportedly visited every one of Scotland's 71 constituencies. There was a concern that she might become over-exposed and the party's national executive felt that she should reduce her broadcast media appearances. An audience research report on the SNP party political broadcast by Ewing on St Andrews Day 1967 on Radio 4 (Scotland) was good news for the party. The small Scottish sample of a questionnaire issued by the BBC's audience research department showed a very positive response. Listeners were asked to rate the broadcast on a scale from A+ to C-.

The BBC had a 'reaction index' that took account of these scores

A+%	A%	B%	C%	C-%
20	32	38	9	1

and gave the broadcast 65. This compared very well with the average of 49 for party political broadcasts.[16]

The problem with this was that many media outlets only wanted Winnie Ewing and turning down such invitations meant there would be no SNP voice.[17] Hamilton was as much Winnie Ewing's personal victory as an SNP victory. There was an element of jealousy amongst some members of the executive. The same attitude would exist a decade later when Margo MacDonald attracted massive media attention and some jealousy within the party. While there was no effort by leading party members to gag Ewing in the late 1960s, as there was with MacDonald a decade later, there was no real strategy and limited understanding of how best to take advantage of this new-found interest in the SNP. At every level, the SNP was on a steep learning curve.

Hamilton's impact on the SNP

The SNP was in exuberant mood even before the end of the campaign. The party's Organisation Committee, meeting on 30 September, heard one senior party member call for a 'tune composed to fit' the slogan, 'SCOTLAND FREE BEFORE '73 – HELP BY JOINING THE SNP'. In large measure, the view was that this mood of optimism was needed to maintain momentum but it was hubristic. The influx of members provided the party with more money and resources enabling it to appoint Donald Bain as full-time research office in 1968 and Douglas Crawford as director of communications the following year. Five days after the by-election there were reports of between 700 and 800 new members in Glasgow and a claim that people were queuing to join at the Glasgow office.[18] As would happen almost half a century later, the surge in members brought problems with it. The Hamilton branch met three weeks after the by-election and, having doubled the membership to 300 from the number at the start of the campaign, required a larger room than normal. There was competition between branches as to which picked up most new members. It was no surprise that Blantyre, in the Hamilton constituency, had gained most members by the end of the year. But Campbeltown in Argyll and Arbroath in Angus, the branch of the Walkers who had honeymooned in Hamilton, also saw massive increases in membership. Hamilton's effect was felt across Scotland.

New SNP branches reported at SNP's 34th annual conference May 1968, Aberdeen			
January 1967	9	October 1967	18
February 1967	13	November 1967	12
March 1967	27	December 1967	23
April 1967	14	January 1968	10
May 1967	10	February 1968	20
June 1967	No report	March 1968	23
July 1967	20	April 1968	28
September 1967	8		

By the time of its May 1968 conference, the SNP had 434 branches. The constituency associations had risen from 26 (of 71 constituencies) at the start of 1967 to 43 at the time of the Hamilton by-election to 60 by the 1968 conference, with a presence of some sort in all constituencies and 17 prospective Parliamentary candidates adopted. It had just under 200 councillors across Scotland and had the infrastructure of a serious political party capable of contesting elections across Scotland. But it was an inexperienced, fragile organisation partly built on the enthusiasm generated by Hamilton rather than the slow progress that leads to deep roots being established in communities.

While the impression might have been that the SNP could carry all before it, there were early signs that it would still be an uphill battle. A young woman candidate standing in an Aberdeen council by-election failed to win the seat a week after Hamilton despite much hype and comparisons with Ewing. It also became clear that the advances made in local elections earlier in the year were creating problems. The Hamilton victory meant that what might have been reported only in the local press attracted attention in Scotland's national papers. In late November, reports were carried of the resignations of three SNP councillors elected six months before in Glenrothes. Family and business commitments had made carrying on as councillors difficult. The party was forced to consider stricter selection procedures and Ewing herself was forced to offer an opinion.[19]

There was another dimension to Hamilton's impact on the SNP that is rarely noted. The election of Winnie Ewing provided an important platform for the SNP to showcase its objectives and values. Those attracted to the party were attracted to an SNP in Winnie Ewing's image. She may not have been leader but, as Gordon Wilson predicted in his 1964 report on the party's reorganisation, as soon as an SNP member became an MP, that person would effectively become party leader. She was the public face of the party and while her role in personifying what the party stood for would be diluted as it gained support in the 1970s, her stamp on the party would remain significant. Her emphatic internationalism and what would now be called multi-culturalism projected an important image. In time, the SNP came to understand which voters were more amenable to its message but Ewing's attitude was that all voters in Scotland – regardless of class, gender, ethnicity or origins – could be won over. The one demographic that the SNP felt it had an especial appeal was youth, reflecting their relative lack of alignment with existing parties. Ewing's appeal was as much based on optimism and aspiration as it was on specific policy positions. While she consistently evaded simple categorisation, she was not unwilling to offer views across a wide range of issues. Her record in the by-election and as Hamilton's MP placed her firmly on the liberal left. Fifty years on, the SNP remains broadly in the same space.

A few people who had been members of the SNP, but who had previously drifted away, returned. In some cases, this took time. Robert Gray, a Progressive Councillor in Glasgow, had been a founding member of the National Party of Scotland and played a part in the removal of Stone of Destiny from Westminster Abbey. He considered joining the party after Hamilton but could see no advantage in standing as an SNP candidate in local elections.[20] Margo MacDonald eventually persuaded him to join the SNP in 1974. Gray, as so many others, was aware of the history of waves of support ebbing away and sought more evidence that Hamilton represented more than another short-term development. Gray and his wife Mary had been close friends of the Ewings, though Mary had irritated Winnie Ewing, the day after the by-election in her capacity as a BBC journalist who had been fairly aggressive interviewing the new MP, no doubt in order to avoid any accusations of favouritism.

Winnie at Westminster

The Hamilton result had an immediate impact in Westminster and Whitehall. It 'put the wind up the rest of Scotland's Labour and Tory MPs', according to one newspaper.[21] The Commons' Order Paper for the day Ewing took up her seat included 98 Parliamentary Questions tabled for the Scottish Office, the highest number on record for any one day. Half of Scotland's Labour MPs had tabled questions, as had four of the 21 Tory MPs and four of the five Liberal MPs, on a vast array of subjects, reflecting the wide responsibilities of the Scottish Office. Treasury officials noted the extra workload as Scottish MPs set out to ask a 'flood of questions'.[22]

The SNP leadership recognised that Winnie Ewing would need support; she would later describe being the sole SNP MP as being a 'terrible responsibility'.[23] Gordon Wilson drew up a plan which included a Parliamentary Advisory panel consisting of Robert McIntyre, Arthur Donaldson, Billy Wolfe and Hugh MacDonald. Lines of communication were agreed with the Glasgow SNP office responsible for publicity and the Edinburgh headquarters – the principal liaison office between Ewing and the party's leadership. An appeal was launched for support in London and discussion of sharing the cost of support in Westminster with Plaid Cymru. Gwynfor Evans, Plaid's MP, and Ewing provided mutual support and each would try to be in the Commons when the other was due to speak. Ewing suffered far more from heckling, but as Evans' biographer noted, her experience as a court lawyer helped her and she taught Evans resolve more than anyone.[24]

Sunday evenings after the by-election would see a small group of advisers meeting at the Ewing's family home in Glasgow to discuss tactics. Michael Grieve would occasionally bring his father Hugh MacDiarmid; Ewing's daughter Annabelle recalls being entertained by and entertaining MacDiarmid. Leading economist David Simpson advised on economic matters. Much of the work was responsive. For example, when the Transport Bill was presented in Parliament at the end of 1967, the SNP sought out expertise to assist. Wolfe collated opinion and evidence that would be sent to Ewing in Parliament.

Ewing chose to give her maiden speech just 96 hours after taking up her seat in a debate on the Latey Report on the Age of Majority.[25] Latey's committee had been asked to consider whether the Age of Majority should be lowered from 21 to 18. Its remit excluded Scotland. Its main recommendation was that the age of full legal capacity and responsibility should be reduced from 21 to 18.[26] The main recommendations were based on an understanding of an 'assessment of the young today, how they live, what they need, what they are like and how mature they are'.[27] The question of the voting age was excluded from the committee's remit but inevitably arose in debates on its findings. Ewing gave two reasons for participating in the debate despite the report's exclusion of Scotland: 'The first is the danger of Scotland being included and the second is the danger of Scotland being excluded'[28] in proposals that followed. Unsuitable afterthought clauses might be added to include Scotland or Scotland might have to wait some time before reforms were extended to Scotland. She pleaded the case for the law to be made simple and easily knowable and saw debate on the voting age as the logical next step. In an interview before the debate, she had said that there should be one age for everything – marriage, drinking, driving, gambling and voting – and that age 'should be 17 or 18' and she favoured 17.[29] She suggested that lowering the voting age would 'hasten the day when I shall be fortunate enough to have some colleagues to join me here from the party I represent'[30] but the thrust of her argument was less partisan self-interest than the application of a legally trained mind to contemporary issues.

Ewing was a very active MP with a high profile for a new MP. She intended to be the most expensive MP by asking lots of Parliamentary Questions. She had her column in the *Daily Record* and each week the *Scottish Daily Express* reported on 'Winnie at Westminster'. There were frequent requests for interviews from television, radio and the press. As noted earlier, this provoked some jealousy amongst her fellow SNP members but nothing like the enmity generated amongst some Labour opponents. She was invited and expected to speak at SNP public meetings throughout Scotland as well as be an active constituency Member.

Ewing was expected to speak for Hamilton but also for Scotland. Any absence from the Commons was criticised by Labour opponents. She responded vigorously, including a letter to the *Scotsman* in which she referred to the 'customary stance of some MPs whilst at the House is closer to the many bars than the Bar of the House'[31] which provoked a formal complaint to the Speaker from a Labour MP. It elevated something that was relatively trivial, as Labour MP Emrys Hughes pointed out, into a matter of national importance. Jock Bruce Gardyne, Tory MP for South Angus, noted that Ewing was on her own in the Commons and it was fair to say that she had been the 'object of a certain campaign of personalised criticism' by some Labour MPs.[32] Her record as a Parliamentarian was impressive by any standards and her presence ensured that other Scottish MPs became much more active.

She had international interests and was active in raising questions about the civil war in Nigeria. Her interests in Africa provoked fury amongst some expatriate Scots in Africa. One South African resident wrote to SNP headquarters complaining about Ewing's voting record and the 'Road to Moscow' elements in the SNP after she opposed selling arms to South Africa.[33] In February 1968, she voted with Gwynfor Evans, the Liberals, Michael Foot and other Labour rebels, and a number of liberal minded Tories against the Commonwealth Immigrants Bill which would exclude Kenyan Asians from British citizenship. The issue has been described as 'among the most divisive and controversial decisions taken by any British government'.[34] Ewing knew there were few votes in Hamilton in her stance. She had talked this through with her husband and agreed that at the next election voters would have to decide whether they wanted an MP or a cypher. Only three Scottish Labour MPs joined her in opposing the Bill at second reading.[35]

It is easy to forget, when reading the correspondence and discussions on how her time should be used, that Ewing had a young family. The demands on her time were exceptional. She preferred to give priority to attending meetings and supporting candidates in local by-elections. Hamilton activists wanted her to spend more time in the constituency. Being an MP was new to Ewing and her party; and she was being pushed and pulled in all directions. Robert McIntyre's brief period as an MP between April and July 1945 was not comparable. While there was considerable expertise in the party across a range of subjects, it was not used to the demands, expectations and levels of scrutiny that came with the by-election result.

By-elections post mortems

Parties conduct post mortems after elections, especially after suffering a devastating defeat. There was little hard evidence to analyse and some interpretations gained currency quickly. The *Hamilton Advertiser* published after the by-election result declared that Labour only had itself to blame for the defeat. The candidate did not have sufficient time to make himself known to the electorate and could not be blamed for the defeat, 'It was lost by the other Mr Wilson at No.10 whose explanations of policy have failed to convince Scots.'[36] Local issues, it maintained, were not important, 'Bings and slums have largely gone. And with them the safest Labour seat in Scotland. An era has ended, a new one begun.'[37]

The elevation of Tom Fraser to a £9,000 per annum public office (from a salary of £3,750 per annum as an MP) might have alienated Labour voters. The Labour Government's difficulties did not help.[38] The decline of the Tory vote might have been because much of that vote was never really a Tory vote at all but the Tory option was the only non-Labour option available to voters at the previous two elections. Whether or not voters supported the SNP because they wanted self-government was unclear.

Some commentaries focused on the candidates, comparing the SNP's 'first class candidate' who represented the 'new social stratum' against the version of 'cloth-cap socialism' who had been foisted on the constituency. Women were thought to have swung it for Ewing with many women who 'came out of political purdah' to vote differently from their husbands for the first time.[39] Janey Buchan, later Scottish Labour chair and MEP, warned against blaming the Labour candidate and argued that two factors swung Hamilton from Labour: the women's vote and high prices.[40] The National Union of Mineworkers (NUM) blamed the defeat on the Wilson Government; Mick McGahey, acting President of the NUM's Scottish area, was not going to allow his union to take the blame for the result and called on the Government to reverse its economic policies.[41]

Within a fortnight of the by-election, Alex Wilson was adopted to stand again for Labour at the next general election. He felt that the party needed a good press agent to 'put him over to the public' and that the party machine needed to be overhauled.[42] But it was not only the local Labour Party that had to address its failings. Hamilton forced its way onto the Labour Government's already crowded agenda. Harold Wilson's problems were mounting. Just over a fortnight after the by-election, Wilson was forced to devalue the pound sterling. In his famous broadcast, he tried to avert a sense of crisis by insisting that the 'pound here in Britain, in your pocket or purse or in your bank, has been devalued' but there was no denying the crisis faced by the Government. James Kellas noted that Labour's 'hatred' of the SNP was 'far greater than their hostility towards the Tories'.[43] Willie Ross described the SNP as a 'phoney party' the day after the by-election,[44] provoking the *Glasgow Herald* to suggest that he had 'not learned the lesson yet' and suggested that Ross was not the best person to take Scotland through these difficult times as he had a 'remarkable capacity for aggravating discontent'.[45] A meeting of Scottish Labour MPs attended by William Marshall, Scottish Secretary of the party, shortly after the by-election was better attended than normal. Reports suggested that Willie Ross was under pressure and being blamed for the result.[46]

In his regular *Daily Record* column after the by-election, Tam Dalyell warned that 'life for the Labour Party in Scotland may not be quite the same again'. He never had any delusions about the potential electoral appeal of the SNP. He said that Ewing would be treated with 'courtesy and a degree of friendliness' but her views would be subject to the 'anvil of critical and informed debate'.[47] He was right on the latter but wrong on the former. Notably, Donald

Stewart, who replaced Ewing as the only SNP MP in 1970, was never treated the same way. In part, this may be explained by gender, in part by Stewart's focus on his constituency and limited part played in campaigning across Scotland and in part because opponents viewed his victory in the Western Isles as less threatening. Dalyell's view was that those who voted SNP in Hamilton and West Lothian did so because the Government was 'far too remote'. He had listened to his Labour colleague John Mackintosh's case for a Scottish Parliament. It was not an endorsement of devolution from the Labour MP who would be one of its leading opponents but an acknowledgement that Labour needed to take the SNP seriously.[48]

Tam Dalyell was one of the few Labour members to have seen the possibility of the SNP taking Hamilton. In his diaries, Richard Crossman records conversations with Dalyell, who served Crossman as his Parliamentary Private Secretary, in which the West Lothian MP predicted that the 'Scot Nat woman might win and the Tories would certainly lose their deposit'. Dalyell had been in the constituency a great deal and told Crossman that Tom Fraser's departure to a well-paid job had 'caused great resentment among the miners'.[49] This had also happened with the by-election on the same day in Leicester South West when Herbert Bowden had resigned to become chair of the Independent Television Authority and a life peer.

Dalyell maintained that canvassing was done only by members from outside the constituency and recounts a conversation with a Labour stalwart of 40 years who was secretary of the largest pensioners' group in Hamilton. She had informed him and John Mackintosh that the former MP Tom Fraser had 'treated us as if were that *cloot* (In Scots, a *cloot* is a cloth used for wiping dirt off dishes). At that moment, Mackintosh and I turned to each other with the same thought: "I doubt Labour's had it"'. This criticism was due to Fraser failing to take part in any farewell event, thanking his constituency for support over his years as MP.[50] It was reported that about 16 Labour MPs had helped out in the by-election[51] but there was little support locally. Labour did not have the troops on the ground. A report in the *New Statesman* described the situation, 'On polling day for each Labour car Mrs Ewing had 20. While Labour workers fussed over out-of-date canvass cards, mini-skirted SNP enthusiasts thrust glamorous photographs of their candidate into electors' hands. Over great areas there were no Labour posters, no photographs of the candidate. It was as if he did not exist. As night fell, anxious supporters, appalled by the absence of Party workers, got down themselves to pulling out the vote – too late.'[52]

Labour responds

On previous occasions when the Scottish Question had come to the fore, Governments had responded by creating and then extending administrative devolution.[53] This would be the case after Hamilton too. There were news reports within days of the by-election of a 'search' for new powers for the Scottish Office.[54] Transport was under discussion at this time with Barbara Castle, Minister of Transport, bringing forward plans for merchant port authorities. A new Scottish Transport Group was proposed in the Transport Bill brought before the Commons at the end of 1967. This attracted considerable attention from Scottish MPs provoking one English MP to complain that the discussion of the Bill had turned into a Scottish Grand Committee debate.[55] There were reports suggesting that Hamilton had assisted Willie Ross in his battle with Barbara Castle to have the Scottish Transport Group under the Scottish Office.[56] The battle had been raging inside Whitehall from well before the by-election but Hamilton gave the Scottish Office greater influence. The nationalised bus service, Clyde steamers and the state's share in MacBrayne's ferries would come under the Scottish Office from 1969.

On the day before the by-election, John Mackintosh suggested that the Scottish Grand Committee – 'as a Parliament within a Parliament'[57] – should meet occasionally in Edinburgh but the idea was dismissed by Willie Ross. The idea of having Scottish Grand Committee meetings in Edinburgh had been around for a long time and the Committee had met in Edinburgh on an experimental basis during the Second World War but there was little appetite amongst Scottish MPs for these meetings. In July, the Liberal MPs led by David Steel had proposed Edinburgh meetings of the Committee along with other minor changes in Parliamentary procedures but found little support. The new post-Hamilton context put it back on the table, but the Scottish Labour Group in the Commons rejected the idea at a meeting in March 1968. Furthermore, they opposed devolving social security, defence and fiscal policy to the Scottish Office but were divided on devolving labour, transport and trade.[58]

Emrys Hughes, Keir Hardie's son-in-law and MP for South Ayrshire, proposed that specialist committees for Scottish affairs should be established. He had argued for specialist committees for Scottish agriculture and housing in March and April.[59] Hamilton gave impetus to his demand.[60] The Scottish executive of the Labour Party gave its unanimous support to the Scottish Parliamentary Labour Group's call for a Select Committee and urged consideration of extending the time that the Scottish Grand Committee met.[61] A Scottish Select Committee was set up in February 1969 and its first enquiry was into the Scottish economy and finance.

Labour had abandoned its support for Scottish home rule in the 1950s, but there remained a small core of home rulers inside the party, including John Mackintosh. He argued for a Scottish Parliament at Glasgow Fabian Society's annual dinner in October, proposing that it should have responsibility for all Scottish Office matters.[62] Reports in the press suggested that the Cabinet was considering home rule for Scotland.[63] In February 1968, Wilson set up a Cabinet Committee to examine devolution. Richard Crossman was one of the supporters of devolution in the Cabinet. He produced a paper setting out two plans: one to be implemented in the next few years and the other over the longer term. The first involved 'educating public opinion on the merits of the present unitary system of government'; further administrative devolution; and 'Parliamentary devolution' involving Welsh and Scottish Grand Committees meeting in Cardiff and Edinburgh respectively. The information for the 'educational' element would be provided by Whitehall. The second longer term plan was to establish a Royal Commission or establish a Scottish National Assembly.[64] Deep divisions inside the Labour Party and Government were addressed with the appointment of a Royal Commission on the Constitution in 1969. This was in part a response to Hamilton but also to the decision by Ted Heath to set up a Conservative Party Committee. It seemed like a good idea to kick the issue into the long grass in the hope that by the time it reported, the issue would have gone away.

The Treasury produced figures to show that Scotland got its fair share of public expenditure in response to a Question from Tory MP Hector Munro. Scotland received more than England per head of population for all but a few items of expenditure. Scotland lagged behind England for law and order items and Selective Employment Tax additional payments but across the gamut of other services for which figures were made available, Scotland appeared to have little to complain about. The extent to which Scotland was subsidised by or subsidised the rest of the UK would become a running theme in Scottish politics thereafter. This debate had surfaced periodically over the 20th century but its intensity and frequency would increase after Hamilton.

Conservative responses

Coming third, especially shortly after gaining Pollok from Labour, was a major jolt for the Scottish Tories. The immediate response from some critics of the leadership focused on abandoning 'Unionist' in the party's name and literature. There were reports suggesting that the use of the 'English term Conservative' had caused difficulties.[65]

The Orange vote was thought to have abandoned the Tories due to the party dropping 'Unionist' from its name. However, a survey conducted for Conservative Central Office had found that amongst Conservatives there was an 'overwhelming preference to be called Conservative rather than Tory or Unionist'. When asked what name was 'most unpleasant', almost half could give no answer but a clear majority of those who did thought *Tory* was the most unpleasant.[66]

George Younger, Ayr's Tory MP, told a conference of Young Conservatives that they ought to welcome the controversy which the SNP brought to Scottish politics. Nothing was 'ever going to be the same again' as Scotland entered a 'most exciting and volatile' situation.[67] The Thistle Group of young Edinburgh University Tory graduates produced a pamphlet arguing for a 'revolution' in the party's organisation in Scotland and devolution from the party in London.[68] Some Tories saw the SNP's advance as creating an opportunity to weaken Labour's emerging grip on Scottish politics. They believed that they could not weaken Labour on their own but the SNP might act as shock troops who would suffer heavy casualties and allow the Tories to pick up the spoils after the Labour–SNP battle was over. But this was little different from the complacent thinking that had started the rot in Tory support. There were a few Tory (and Labour) defectors to the SNP at local level and much speculation about others.

A report in March 1968 on the rising tide of nationalism was prepared for Conservative Central Office. The 'bad image' of the party in Scotland gave it a 'pretty gloomy' long term outlook, according to Head of Communications.[69] Copies were sent to the party's Scottish chair warning him that it did 'not make very happy reading'.[70] The party's image was widely debated internally. Ted Heath addressed the 1968 Scottish Tory conference in May with his 'Declaration of Perth', an allusion to the 1320 'Declaration of Arbroath'. Heath set up a Scottish Constitutional Committee under former Prime Minister Lord Home to look at the details and committed his party to some form of elected devolution. Home's committee reported in March

1970, the day of the South Ayrshire by-election. It recommended a 125 member 'Scottish Convention' directly elected by Scottish voters. There were two dissenting voices on the committee but many more amongst Tory MPs, including Shadow Scottish Secretary Michael Noble, and many activists were unhappy with the proposals. There was a sense that the party had been pushed into supporting devolution in a knee-jerk response to the rise of the SNP. But the SNP threat appeared to have lessened considerably by the time Home's Committee had reported. The 1970 Tory manifesto proposed that the Home Report's proposals would 'form the basis for the proposals we will place before Parliament'.[71] But press reports of splits inside the Conservative Party meant that even those who supported an elected assembly did not expect one to be established by Heath.[72]

Liberals

A few days after Hamilton, John Bannerman, President of the Scottish Liberals, once more returned to the question of a pact with the SNP. While accepting that there was no prospect of this being agreed at national level, he suggested that conflict between the two parties should be averted at constituency level. He warned that otherwise there would be no voice for Scotland and argued that the electorate could not understand 'any difference in the intensity of Scottishness' in separate SNP and Liberal voices.[73] Bannerman also took up a seat in the Lords a few days after Hamilton and referred to the 'anger of Hamilton' as the 'symbol of widespread Scottish anger at the misgovernment from Whitehall' in his maiden speech. He argued that there was a 'swelling anger of Scotsmen through two centuries of time' and made the case for federalism across Britain.[74]

The idea of cooperation with the Liberals was given further voice by Liberal leader Jeremy Thorpe. Thorpe gave Ewing support from the moment she entered the Commons as an act of personal decency. In coded language designed to avoid upsetting his Scottish colleagues who opposed any deal, Thorpe hinted at the prospect of the Liberals standing aside for the SNP in central Scotland while the SNP gave the Liberals a free run in the Highlands and Borders.[75] But the SNP rejected the idea of a pact. James Davidson, Liberal MP for West Aberdeenshire, introduced a bill to allow a referendum on devolution and Jo Grimond called for a referendum on a Scottish Television programme.[76] The SNP was happy to support this but there was no support beyond the SNP and Liberals for a referendum. Having been lonely voices making the case for home rule, the Liberals were in danger of being eclipsed.

Gorbals and South Ayrshire

Five by-elections were held on the same day across Britain at the end of October 1969, including one in Glasgow Gorbals. Labour lost one of the five seats and came uncomfortably close in three. Only in Gorbals could Labour take comfort from the result. Alice Cullen, Labour MP since a by-election in 1948, had died. Frank McElhone, a local fruiterer, was Labour's standard bearer. The SNP won a quarter of the votes but Labour won over half. Rehousing and the lack of boundary changes since 1955, meant the number of people living in the constituency had shrunk. Housing was the dominant issue in the by-election. Labour poured resources and effort into the by-election intent on 'bursting the Nationalist bubble'.[77] All the SNP could claim from the result was that it was the main opposition to Labour in Scotland, a not inconsiderable claim compared with a decade before if true but a long way from Scotland being 'free by 73'.[78] A *Glasgow Herald* editorial warned that it was the SNP's 'misfortune' that another by-election was pending in South Ayrshire, another Labour stronghold, in which they would have to do well if they hoped to make an impact at the imminent general election.[79]

The South Ayrshire by-election was held in March 1970 following the death of Emrys Hughes who had been one of the few Scottish

Labour MPs to engage constructively with and treat Winnie Ewing with courtesy. The Liberals did not stand a candidate. Jo Grimond, who had been put in charge of the party's Scottish general election campaign, had been keen on a pact with the SNP and the party allowed the SNP a free run.[80] According to an SNP activist and parliamentary candidate, it was the most bruising contest witnessed in about half a century of political activity. Sam Purdie, the SNP candidate, had been former Labour MP Emrys Hughes' election agent, adding to a sense of betrayal amongst Labour members. The SNP won only 20.4 per cent of the vote, and came third behind Labour and the Conservatives. Sillars' majority of 10,886 had been, as the *Glasgow Herald* declared, a 'tremendous victory'.[81] Labour could go into the 1970 general election in Scotland with confidence. This was the first election in Scotland at which 18 year olds had a vote and while the SNP claimed to have captured this younger age group, the signs were that lowering the voting age had not damaged Labour. In 1968, Jim Sillars, Labour's South Ayrshire candidate, co-authored an anti-devolution pamphlet that attacked the SNP, 'Don't Butcher Scotland's Future'.[82] Sillers and Wilie Ross shared a reputation as the 'Hammer of the Nats'.[83] Sillars' views would evolve and having entered Parliament as a staunch Unionist, he would breakaway from Labour to form his own Scottish Labour Party and eventually join the SNP.

An opinion poll published the day after the by-election suggested that the SNP would find itself in third place in Hamilton at the general election. Strathclyde University's Survey Research Centre suggested that Labour would win 43 per cent; Conservatives 28 per cent and SNP 21 per cent with 8 per cent Don't Knows.[84] Further research was reported the following week drawing on other surveys in Glasgow, Stirling, Rutherglen with more bad news for the SNP. Under the headline, 'SNP unlikely to appear in next Parliament', it suggested that the SNP would win 20 per cent across Scotland. Its best hope was that it would do well 'in a constituency cut off from the general political trends of Central and Southern Scotland.'[85] The survey showed the

SNP polling strongest amongst council house tenants. SNP support in Glasgow was coming nine times more heavily from Labour than the Tories; five times more in Stirling; and seven times more in Hamilton. Support for independence was 'meagre' though relatively high in Glasgow: 43 per cent in Glasgow supported independence; 19 per cent in Stirling; 9 per cent in Rutherglen; and 21 per ent in Hamilton.[86]

Public opinion

Opinion polls in Scotland were conducted more often after Hamilton. They show that the the SNP support ebbed away by the time of the 1970 general election. In addition, there were the results of local elections which confirmed the general impression created by the polls.

'How would you vote if there were a General Election tomorrow?' [sample size of 200 for Scotland recorded for Nov 1968]

	Cons %	Lab %	Liberal %	Nationalist %	Other %
1966 General Election	37.5	49.8	6.8	5.0	0.9
November 1967	25	41	9	24	1
December 1967	25.3	38.7	7.7	28.3	
February-April 1968 (3 surveys combined)	25	41	9	24	1
May 1968	30	22	4	43	1
June 1968	29.2	32.5	5.5	32.2	0.6
January 1969	33.5	39.3	5.7	20.9	0.6
March 1970	43.0	37.5	6.5	12.5	0.5
General Election 1970	38.0	44.5	5.5	11.4	0.4

Sources: National Opinion Polls Ltd Bulletin; Kellas 1971, p.455.

Other polls were conducted on Scotland's constitutional status. These were often crude and of limited value in understanding public opinion but they fed the appetite for news and encouraged the view that change was imminent. Some polls were sensational but of dubious validity such as the one reported below. Dr Jack Brand, director of the Survey Research Centre at Strathclyde University, summing up the result, said that Nationalist movement still had to reach a peak in Scottish politics.'

SEPARATISM As in the Irish Republic, Scotland would be a wholly separate and sovereign nation, with its own tax system. Treasury, Foreign Policy, communications system	79.92%
FEDERALISM	8.74%
SCOTTISH ASSEMBLY	5.64%
STRONGER CIVIL SERVICE	0.62%
NO CHANGE	5.08%

Scots Independent, 1 June 1968 from *Daily Record*, nd.

As local elections were held each year before the reorganisation of local government in the 1970s, it is possible to track support in actual votes though care needs to be take in interpreting these results. The Conservatives commonly contested local elections under a variety of names or as Independents though not all Independents were Tories.

The SNP experienced a post-Hamilton surge in support but was unable to sustain this through to the general election but where it ended up was considerably higher than it had been at the previous general election.

	1966 %	1967 %	1968 %	1969 %	1970 %
Labour	49.6	41.8	33.0	36.9	50.3
Conservative/ Right-wing	46.0	39.8	32.9	37.3	35.2
SNP	4.4	18.4	34.1	25.8	14.5
	100.0	100.0	100.0	100.0	100.0

Source: Iain McLean, 'The Rise and fall of the Scottish National Party', *Political Studies*, vol.18, 1970, p.362.

1970 General Election

The SNP went into the 1970 general election expecting to advance but knowing it would be tough. Hamilton was lost but Ewing came in second with 35 per cent, well behind Alex Wilson for Labour on 53 per cent but well ahead of Ross Harper for the Tories on 11 per cent. It fell back in West Lothian to below its share of the vote in 1966 or 1964 but polled relatively strongly in north-east Scotland and the Highlands, picking up Liberal support. It was a gloomy night for the SNP until the final result was declared in the Western Isles where Donald Stewart, Provost of Stornoway, took the seat from Labour. He had been on the wish list of candidates, along with Winnie Ewing, discussed by the SNP's Election Committee in 1962. Reflecting on the results, Kellas suggested that Hamilton had been a 'totally isolated oasis for the SNP'.[87] The SNP lost 43 deposits contesting 65 seats, with its average vote in seats contested falling from 14.5 per cent to 12.2 per cent compared with 1966. But, it was contesting many more seats and places it had not had any organisation or much of a membership in four years before.

Heath abandoned his commitment to an elected Assembly. Lord Crowther, the chair of the Royal Commission told Heath that he had 'no illusions about the reasons for setting up' the Commission and there would be 'no ill feelings' if Heath wound up the Commission.[88] But Commission carried on. Crowther died and was replaced by Lord Kilbrandon and the report was published in late 1973. The timing was fortuitous for the SNP as it coincided with the Govan by-election. It generated considerable attention. Margo MacDonald, another charismatic woman and highly articulate SNP candidate, was able to tap into the mood. A Royal Commission that had been set up to remove the issue of home rule from the agenda ended up boosting interest in it and support for the SNP.

Conclusion

Parties welcome surges in membership and support but a surge is like a wave that flows but will ultimately ebb. What is left after the surge is unclear. The SNP's Hamilton surge had ebbed by the time of the 1970 general election but the SNP was in a much stronger position than it had been before Hamilton, though the heady expectations were not realised. Far more important was the far greater focus on the Scottish Question on the part of the SNP's opponents. The surge gave confidence to key supporters of home rule beyond the SNP, especially in the press, as well as inside the Labour Party. Increased sensitivity to Scottish interests in Whitehall and Westminster ensured that there was far greater attention to Scotland. But it would take another advance before the SNP forced devolution firmly onto the agenda. Equally important, and perhaps least acknowledged in subsequent commentary, was Winnie Ewing's articulation of Scottish nationalism as a liberal internationalist cause which became standard for the SNP.

CONCLUSION

Hamilton in a Historical Context

> What happened between the late '50s and the early '70s has been subject to political polemic, nostalgic mythologising, and downright misrepresentation.[1]

> If you remember the '60s, you really weren't there.[2]

> The effect of this [the SNP's Hamilton by-election victory] was immediate, and shattering to the established order... this was a brave, defiant gesture in the supposed tradition of Scotland's past... SNP had made a big noise, and in politics a big noise is often heard. It was indeed heard throughout the world, and in Scotland itself it stunned most of the practical (and academic) politicians into silence.[3]

> ... Without doubt, Hamilton was one of a handful of by-elections in the 20th century which really mattered in the long term.[4]

Flower of Scotland

PIPPA NORRIS distinguished between two schools of thought in her study of by-elections: the conventional view that by-elections were 'campaign-specific', as 'idiosyncratic contests reflecting the strengths and weaknesses of individual candidates and local party organisations' vs the 'referendum' thesis which views by-elections offering systematic evidence of the relative strength of parties and therefore like opinion polls except they are 'real'.[5] She concluded that neither view is 'entirely satisfactory'.[6] An article in the *Glasgow Herald* asked whether Hamilton was the start of a political trend culminating in a Scottish Nationalist majority of Scottish MPs or a 'tartan' Orpington with no further significance.[7] Analysis of by-elections over the period 1945–87 suggested that minor parties tend to gain at the expense of the party in government and by-elections can indicate long-term trends in public opinion. As the electorate became less inclined to associate strongly with one of the two main parties, this gave rise to more volatility especially at by-elections. But by-elections, especially held mid-term of a Parliament, are poor guides as to the outcome of the next general election.[8]

The SNP's Hamilton victory did not come out of nowhere. There was nothing inevitable about the Hamilton result or its impact. There had been stirrings well before November 1967. Arnold Kemp, editor of the (*Glasgow*) *Herald*, was working at the *Scotsman* when the paper's political editor came on the line seconds after the Hamilton declaration. He recounted the 'mood of excitement'. Hamilton 'launched the SNP into the stratosphere of concentrated London media attention and from [Ewing's] victory is often traced the party's prominence. But Hamilton was not the beginning. It was the flowering.'[9] Kemp's portrayal of Hamilton as a flowering captures well the developments before the by-election as well as the nature of the victory.

The excitement generated by the result went well beyond the SNP and included people who might never vote for the party. Reports that Scottish Office civil servants based in Dover House, London were jubilant on hearing the result, provoked Tam Dalyell to ask Willie Ross the rhetorical Parliamentary Question, 'whether it was with his authority that officials of his Department sent a congratulatory telegram from Dover House to the Hon Member for Hamilton on Friday, 3 November'. Ross replied that he was confident that no senior official would 'forget his professional code' and he did not intend to conduct an interrogation.[10] Hamilton tapped into a mood that went beyond support for independence or home rule.

Its impact on Scottish politics was greater than any previous or subsequent by-election in the 20th century, even the 1963 Kinross and West Perthshire by-election at which the Tory candidate was Prime Minister Alec Douglas-Home. Hamilton provoked a reaction in government, across parties and in the media that gave the SNP credibility and a base to build upon. There would not have been the same reaction if Labour had held the seat through a close result. Even a good second place for the SNP would only have been a reprieve for Labour. The impact on the SNP was immense. Winnie Ewing articulated a brand of nationalism that the SNP stuck with subsequently. She would occasionally question whether *nationalism* was an accurate or helpful term, especially in her years as a Member of the European Parliament.[11] Her internationalism was offended by suggestions that she was parochial because she was a 'nationalist'. The SNP would later describe itself as civic and multi-cultural but the ideas had been given more prominence on platforms in Hamilton than ever before and took root inside the party.

Explaining Hamilton 1967

Various explanations have been offered for the result, often reflecting contemporary concerns. A common explanation, especially after the SNP failed to live up to its own hype in the 1970 general election, was that Hamilton had been a protest vote, merely signalling criticism of the Labour Government.[12] A protest vote implies that voters are not voting *for* something but registering opposition and that they will return to the party they would normally vote for at the next election. This has been common in by-election. Most by-election defeats are over-turned at the subsequent general elections. By-elections offer an easy way to protest without bringing down a government.

Such protest vote interpretations of Hamilton emphasised the negative motives for voting SNP and reject the SNP vote as signalling support for independence or home rule. There is reason to find this convincing. The Labour Government struggled with unemployment, emigration and other major economic challenges. There was much to protest against, especially following Labour's election promises of a better future which failed to materialise. The Labour Party was publicly divided on key issues with some local MPs being highly critical of the

Government. Peggy Herbison, well respected MP for a neighbouring seat, stood down from the front bench in 1967 complaining that the Government had failed to do enough for the poor. The SNP campaign emphasised these Labour failings. Unemployment, emigration and the economic challenges were emphasised in SNP literature and speeches. Protest was no doubt part of the explanation but this still leaves questions unanswered. Why was the SNP the beneficiary in Hamilton when the Tories already had a presence in the constituency and had taken seats from Labour in Cambridge and Walthamstow West the previous month as well as winning Leicester South West and coming close in Manchester Gorton on the same day as Hamilton?

A protest vote is a temporary, or at least intermittent, phenomenon. It was commonly assumed that this was the case when the SNP failed to make the breakthrough expected in the 1970 general election but a party's own hype is a poor measure of success. Just as the SNP had misinterpreted Hamilton as signalling that Scotland would be 'free by 73', so did their opponents misinterpret the SNP's defeat in Hamilton and failure to win a single mainland seat at the general election. Winning one vote in ten across Scotland in 1970 compared with one in twenty in 1966 can only be viewed as a relative success. The party won its first seat at a general election and fielded almost three times more candidates than four years before. Again, we return to the question of how we measure success. Measured against expectations that the SNP set itself, 1970 was a setback, but by other measures it was an advance. What is clear from the vantage point of half a century is that the SNP's advance was a slow, uneven and far from certain process.

In the late 1960 and early 1970s, consideration was given to 'relative deprivation' explanations. Relative deprivation is the 'perceived discrepancy between what people think they should achieve and what they have indeed achieved.'[13] This suggests that Scots felt relatively economically aggrieved and had found a means of rectifying the grievance. A key work in the early 1970s argued that an organisation was needed to mobilise the sense of relative deprivation.[14] It was not enough that a community was or perceived itself to be relatively deprived but there needed to be an alternative vision and an organisation making the case and mobilising support. Runciman, in his classic work on relative deprivation, argued that four conditions needed to be met: people need to be deprived of something; know that others have it; they must want it; and believe it can be obtained.[15] There would need to be evidence that each of these conditions existed.

In 1969, the future Scottish Office Chief Economist Gavin McCrone argued that 'recent political developments in Scotland are closely connected with the state of the economy'.[16] We might expect that an economist would look for economic explanations and McCrone provides ample objective evidence of Scotland's relatively weak economic position and reason for voters to seek a means of expressing dissatisfaction. That would satisfy a protest vote explanation. Voters would need to believe that Scotland was deprived compared with other parts of the UK, that this deprivation was unwarranted and that the SNP was the political vehicle with the solution and succeed in mobilising support if relative deprivation explained the SNP's rise.

The absence of opinion survey data from Hamilton limits our ability to test almost any explanation of the Hamilton result but subsequent Scottish public opinion research and the attitudes of leading SNP figures calls relative economic deprivation into question.[17] A study in the early 1970s considered the extent to which Scots felt relatively deprived in five ways: the sufficiency of Parliamentary representation, job opportunities, discrepancies between Scottish and English standards of living, economic positions, and 'style of living'. It concluded that the evidence was far from overwhelming.[18] That does not rule out some aspects of relative deprivation. Most likely, voters were well aware of Scotland's relative economic weakness, not least as this was something Scottish Labour MPs including Hamilton's erstwhile MP had frequently made much of, but it is unclear whether voters believed that this situation could be changed or, most notably, that the SNP had the answers. Subsequent research suggests that while the SNP message consistently complained about the state of the Scottish economy, lack of opportunities for Scots and the high levels of emigration, there is less evidence that this was reflected in attitudes of SNP supporters.[19] It is not unknown for parties and their voters to diverge in their attitudes, views and policy preferences. But it seems unlikely that these criticisms did not have some impact not least as they were shared by many people who did not vote SNP. The SNP campaign also included an upbeat message in Hamilton. Contemporary informed speculation suggested that amongst those who were attracted to Winnie Ewing's message were those who were younger, politically more footloose and optimistic. SNP voters were not necessarily jobless and / or intending to emigrate to Australia.

Context and opportunity

No single factor explains why the SNP won but the combination of context and opportunity, capacity and credibility played their part. Norwegian political scientist Stein Rokkan maintained that a 'cultural base and economic catalyst provide a base for [nationalist] mobilisation'.[20] A cultural base alone is not enough and there is little doubt that there was a distinct Scottish cultural base long before the SNP advance. Again, we do not have solid empirical evidence from surveys of public opinion in 1967 but enough indirect evidence that people living in Scotland saw themselves as Scottish. Key institutions ensured that this identity was transmitted from one generation to the next. A survey reported in the *Glasgow Herald* in 1970 found that 78 per cent of people in Scotland considered themselves Scots and only 18 per cent considered themselves British. Notably, this did not equate with support for the SNP as the same poll suggested SNP support at only 16 per cent. But a cultural base clearly existed in 1970 and presumably would have been similarly strong three years before. Opinion in the 1970 survey was pretty evenly split as to whether

English people were 'much the same or different from Scottish people'.[21] We need to take care and not assume that a cultural identity implies a political (or economic) identity. Feeling Scottish was not enough on its own but it was a prerequisite. So, what was the catalyst and was it economic? Part of the explanation is linked to the 1960s.

As discussed in Chapter One, many scholars thought that modernisation would lead to identities such as Scottish identity being marginalised. When this did not happen and nationalist and regionalist movements grew, the explanation offered was that these movements were defensive in the face of modernising forces. An alternative explanation, suggested here, is that processes of modernisation and the sense of change were embraced by and worked in tandem with the Scottish national movement. From this interpretation, the SNP in Hamilton was not a throw-back or reaction to rapid changes. Indeed, the traditionalism threatened by modernisation was old-fashioned Labour traditionalism. Labour was the small 'c' conservative party. The SNP campaign was modern, carnivalesque, upbeat and positive. The tendency has been to interpret the vitality of the SNP campaign as successful in drawing attention to the party but the campaign style may also have captured a mood in the 1960s at least amongst that section of the population that wanted to embrace change. The SNP's medium may have been as important as its message. The message was more mixed, with negative attacks on Labour combined with the promise of a positive future but the upbeat and modern means of its expression was key.

There was evidence of a mood of hope and change taking place across many liberal democracies in the 1960s. Hamilton was not an island cut off from the rest of the world and voters would have been aware of these changes. The '60s might have provoked a backlash against change but some voters would have wanted to be part of the change represented by the SNP. Harold Wilson had tapped into it in the first half of the 1960s. His positive, progressive and modern message up to 1966 contrasted with what his Government was able to deliver and Labour's message in Hamilton in 1967. This contrast is likely to have helped the SNP, allowing it to pick up Wilson's mantle, discarded by a Prime Minister struggling to deliver on his promises and never embraced by the local Labour Party. The ease with which the SNP was able to adopt a modern, progressive message was aided by a candidate who was its epitome. Winnie Ewing was the antithesis of the kind of old-fashioned politicians that Hamilton was used to electing. Three decades after the by-election, the local paper's chief reporter in 1967 considered her to have had similar qualities to the dominant figure in British politics at the later time. Ewing had been 'articulate and charismatic, a female Tony Blair who shared the aspirations of an emerging "Middle Scotland"'.[22] The comparison ends there but it is an intriguing possibility. Without overstating the comparison, the suggestion was that there was something about Winnie Ewing, as Tony Blair later, that captured the public mood and the sense of a time for change.[23]

Another explanation that has been offered for the SNP's rise was the decline of the British Empire. There is little doubt that this was part of the backdrop but coincidence is not the same as cause. Again, without opinion survey evidence we are left with indirect evidence. The notion that the SNP was an anti-colonial movement has rightly been dismissed. It did not purport to be such and there is no evidence that Scotland saw itself as a colony, internal or otherwise. But a more subtle and convincing argument has been proposed by Nielsen and Ward.[24] They note the main theme in the SNP literature in Hamilton was the 'London government's failure to address the issues of particular importance to Scotland'.[25] Their global focus leads them to consider whether Scottish nationalism was part of the rise of a 'new nationalism' that swept across much of the world in the 1960s. The key characteristics of this new nationalism were the 'dwindling purchase of a universal Britishness as a unifying principle' which arrived along with the decline of Empire and with material and political grievances due to the metropolitan centre's failure to deliver.

This new nationalism manifested itself differently across the world and, intriguingly, without much reference to what was happening elsewhere.[26] This was linked the social and political turbulence in the 1960s. Old allegiances, values and attitudes were challenged during the swinging '60s.

Drawing on contemporary explanations and more recent research, we can now propose *part of* the explanation for the SNP success in Hamilton and its advance in the 1960s. The context will always be an important though insufficient explanation. The 1960s were a period of political and social turbulence. A new nationalism was emerging beyond Scotland and it would be surprising if it had not found voice in Scotland too. Scotland was relatively economically less well off than its neighbour but a more convincing explanation is that voters perceived Scotland as relatively *politically* deprived – it lacked an effective voice in the UK system of government.[27] This sits more comfortably with what we know about earlier developments in Scottish politics. Every generation has had to confront the Scottish Question, the relationship between Scotland and London/ rest of the UK. The demand for a Scottish Office in the late 19th century was followed throughout the 20th century with demands for policies (and more public money) to take account of Scotland's special circumstances. Economic weaknesses fed this sense of relative *political* deprivation. The demand was for an effective political voice. Winnie Ewing's message was emphatically that she would be that voice – promising to become the most expensive MP by asking more questions than any other, ensuring the voices of Hamilton and Scotland would be heard loudly and persistently. Not only did she succeed in this but provoked political opponents to do the same. The demand for self-government that led to victory was then inchoate but in time it would take on a more developed form. The key is that Scottish nationalism in the 1960s was the expression of relative political deprivation.

Capacity and credibility

While the context is undoubtedly important in the development of any political movement, there needs to be political leadership and organisational capacity to mobilise support. The SNP's main achievement in the 1950s was its survival. This might seem a modest achievement but it was important. The party's inability to contest seats limited its ability to learn lessons from experience. But the relentless optimism of SNP activists ensured that a shell of an organisation existed when times improved. Much institutional learning occurred over the 1960s. The party was an amateur activist party, relying on people who worked full-time, often discouraged by employers from political involvement. David Rollo, SNP Treasurer from 1953–1965 and Hamilton candidate in 1959, exemplifies this. Joined by a new generation of activists in the 1960s attracted by advances in West Lothian and Pollok, these were the foot soldiers who kept the faith and travelled to Hamilton over the long by-election. Many members brought professional skills in media and marketing but mostly they brought enthusiasm. The enthusiasm of activists could easily be dissipated but the SNP in Hamilton was fortunate in having John McAteer as its election agent. McAteer knew how to channel this amateur enthusiasm. He knew the constituency well and worked tirelessly.

Minutes of meetings of the national executive and the various national committees show the learning process from earlier political skirmishes that took place. Political post mortems were held before the party moved on to the next battle. West Lothian had taught the importance of having a well-functioning organisation at constituency level and knowing the local issues. Pollok taught lessons in organising at sub-constituency level, the importance of early mobilisation of activists and further honed the party's media strategy. It is unclear the extent to which a conscious effort was made to ensure that the campaign was fun but this appears to have been an important feature that encouraged activists to return and contributed to a sense of community. Winnie Ewing was, without doubt, key to victory. One local activist was unimpressed on first seeing the candidate emerging from her sports car shortly after her nomination. Ewing did not appear likely to be able to relate to Hamilton's working class voters. But the same activist was soon disabused of this first impression and realised that Ewing was an exceptional candidate, one who enjoyed campaigning and was able to relate to people of all backgrounds. Her campaign style and energy became legendary in the SNP.

The SNP managed to make a convincing case that it was a credible alternative to Labour because of advances at previous elections and the high profile nature of its campaign. There was no Liberal candidate and the Tories had never done well in Hamilton. Selective memory of earlier by-election performances allowed the SNP to convince itself that it could win. Indeed, Winnie Ewing herself maintained that believing that victory was possible was important. There were many senior members who believed that the SNP would do well but not win, but Ewing felt that a belief in victory was itself necessary for victory. She managed to convey this belief to activists and Hamilton voters, if not many journalists.

The SNP was helped by the length of the campaign. Rumours that a by-election was imminent started to circulate shortly after the 1966 general election and the SNP started campaigning that summer. Labour may have held off after Plaid Cymru won the Carmarthen by-election in July 1966, fearing another upset north of the border. But postponement only gave the SNP time to campaign. While the SNP's Hamilton campaign was the culmination of years of learning, it would be wrong to ignore the lamentable state of the local Labour Party and Labour's poor campaign. Labour's candidate has often been blamed but the candidate was more a manifestation of Labour's weakness than its cause. In other contexts, he could expect to win, as happened at the three general elections after the by-elections. Labour learned an important lesson and were determined not to make that mistake again.

After Hamilton

After Hamilton, politics in Scotland would be viewed through a Scottish lens by all parties seeking support north of the border. This did not mean that a British perspective was abandoned or marginalised, only that it would always be important to consider whether a Scottish dimension might be appropriate. The warning from the (Balfour) Royal Commission on Scottish Affairs, quoted in chapter one, had not been heeded by successive governments in the decade after the report was published. 'History shows that misunderstandings due to thoughtlessness, lack of tact and disregard of sentiment can be serious.'[28] Immediately after Hamilton, there was a hyper-sensitivity to Scottish grievances across Whitehall. Scottish MPs, spurred into action by Hamilton, made sure of this. There is no agreement as to whether concessions appease or feed nationalist demands but there is little doubt that the Scottish distinctiveness was more widely acknowledged after Hamilton. Within a fortnight, demands were being made for a Scottish Ombudsman. An article in the press complained that the office of Ombudsman in Scotland was merely a branch office.[29] It is unlikely that such an article would have been written had there been a poor showing for the SNP. There would be arguments amongst students of politics whether or not a Scottish political system existed, as would be argued in a seminal book by James Kellas first published in 1973[30] but little doubt about the sense that a distinct Scottish dimension existed.

The SNP's optimism saw it through difficult times but also created problems for the party. Disillusionment followed unchecked optimism and could lead to recriminations. Hamilton was important in the nature of nationalism that was espoused. There were tensions over whether it should steer a left of centre line, a middle course or that it should be above divisive class politics. There were tensions over Europe, though that would become clearer later, but the party's multi-culturalism and internationalism can be accredited to Winnie

Ewing in Hamilton as much as anyone else. It would be embarrassed by elements that had different views but there was never much doubt about the SNP's core beliefs in this respect.

Winnie Ewing personified the SNP in many ways. Despite being defeated in 1970, she went on to create another upset when she defeated Gordon Campbell, the Secretary of State for Scotland, in February 1974 in Moray but lost the seat in 1979. A month later she took the Highlands and Islands constituency in the first direct elections to the European Parliament and was elected as a regional list Member of the newly created Scottish Parliament in 1999. As its oldest Member, she opened the first democratically elected Scottish Parliament in 1999. She remains the only person to have been elected to the House of Commons, European and Scottish Parliaments. Though formally never the party's leader, she held the honorary position of SNP president from 1987–2005. But her role as candidate in Hamilton is likely to be her most important political legacy. Major political phenomena are rarely rooted in a single cause. Hamilton 1967 owed much to the 1960s context and the organisational flair of John McAteer and the SNP's institutional learning but if a single factor had to be identified as the key ingredient to understand the victory then it would have to be Winnie Ewing. She was the fulcrum. She personified a message that was both rooted in Scottish identity and distinctly modern and relevant. Her formidable campaigning skills and energy, self-belief and belief in the likely success of her campaign were crucial to the success.

Politics and society in the 1960s were in a state of flux. Old orthodoxies were being challenged and there were moments, including Hamilton, when much that had been taken for granted had to be re-assessed. This political and social turbulence was linked to economic dislocation, much as it is today. Then, as now, it was difficult to know how politics and society might settle. It was not clear whether a party which had emerged almost from nowhere, or so it seemed to many, might be a passing phase or lead to a major realignment in politics or even the break-up of a polity. What was clear was that the socio-political context created conditions for change but it took exceptionally able political leadership, drawing as much on energy as experience, to take advantage of these conditions. Established parties, lumbering in their response to the new context and political upstarts, preferred the comfort on known misery to the new challenges posed by social and economic change.

Today's Scottish National Party has roots that back into the inter-war period, but its most significant breakthrough, and the path which it has subsequently followed, can be found in the Hamilton by-election. Its civic nationalism and moderate left of centre position allied with an optimism and ability to see opportunities in the most unlikely situations have been its hallmarks over the last 50 years. It would have its obituary written time and time again and indeed would drift in and out of relevance but never disappear. The language that the SNP uses to describe itself today may have changed but the essential ideas remain the same as when Winnie Ewing articulated them in Hamilton. The role of women in politics and society, relations with the rest of Europe, and responding to rapid social and economic beyond the control of any government or party were presaged in Hamilton 50 years ago and remain relevant today. In Hamilton in 1967, it displayed a confidence that infuriated its opponents, challenged orthodoxies and unsettled patterns of behaviour. The SNP was the *upstart* of Scottish politics then and now struggles with its recent status as upstart *and* establishment, operating in an equally unsettled political and economic environment.

Endnotes

Timeline

1 Between 1918 and 1985, candidates had to deposit £150 which was paid back if over one-eighth (12.5%) of the vote was won. The deposit was increased to £500 and the proportion of the vote required to be won to secure the deposit was reduced to one-twentieth (5%). £150 in 1967 would be the equivalent of £1,903 in 2017.

Introduction

1 Pippa Norris, *British By-Elections: The Volatile Electorate*, Oxford, Clarendon Press, 1990, p.28.
2 Jack Brand, *The Nationalist Movement in Scotland*, London, Routledge & Kegan Paul, 1978, p.262.
3 *Daily Record*, 3 November 1967.
4 I am grateful to Ruth and Tam Walker for the information they gave me, including a copy of the newsletter, about their involvement in the campaign.
5 James Kellas, *The Scottish Political System*, Cambridge, Cambridge University Press. The first edition was published in 1973. It had four editions.

Chapter One

1 Harold Wilson, Labour Party annual conference, Scarborough, 1 October 1963.
2 Samuel Huntington, 'The Change to Change', *Comparative Politics*, vol. 3, 1971, p.289.
3 Peter Pulzer, *Political Representation and Elections in Britain*, London, Allen & Unwin, 1967, p.98.
4 *Glasgow Herald*, 19 December 1949. John MacCormick argued that 'Until we have got 3,00,000 signatures we shall not have shown it [that the majority of Scots want home rule]'. The Scottish electorate at the 1950 election was only 3,370,190 and only 2,726,684 voted.
5 Report of the Royal Commission on Scottish Affairs (Balfour), Edinburgh, HMSO, 1954, p.12, para.14.
6 *Glasgow Herald*, 8, 9 July 1959.

7 *Scots Independent*, 5 May 1962.

8 *Hamilton Advertiser*, 12 May 1967.

9 *Hamilton Advertiser*, 6 January 1967.

10 Alec Cairncross, *The Wilson Years: A Treasury Diary 1964–1969*, London, The Historians' Press, 1997, pp.186–191.

11 Ibid., p.191.

12 Toothill, J. N., *Report on the Scottish Economy 1960–1961: Report of a Committee Appointed by the Scottish Council (Development and Industry) under the Chairmanship of J.N. Toothill*, Edinburgh, Scottish Council (Development and Industry), 1961.

13 Gavin McCrone, *Scotland's Future: The Economics of Nationalism*, Oxford, Basil Blackwell, 1969, pp.42–43.

14 Jimmi Østergaard Nielsen and Stuart Ward, '"Cramped and Restricted at Home?" Scottish Separatism at Empire's End', *Transactions of the Royal Historical Society*, vol.25, 2015, p.177.

15 *Hansard*, House of Commons, 31 July 1961, vol.645, col.928–931.

16 Quoted in Anne Deighton, 'The past in the present: British imperial memories and the European question', in Jan-Werner Müller (ed.), *Memory & Power in Post-War Europe: Studies in the presence of the past*, Cambridge, Cambridge University Press, 2002, p.108.

17 *Guardian*, 1 May 1967.

18 *Daily Record*, October 28, 1967.

19 *Glasgow Herald*, 24 May 1948.

20 NLS Papers Acc.9588, George M Lawson papers, Confidential Labour Party RD.347, November 1962 'Working Party on Scottish Policy'.

21 Ibid.

22 Ibid.

23 *Scottish Daily Express*, 28 July 1967.

24 *Scottish Daily Express*, 29 July 1967.

25 Gordon Wilson, *Pirates of the Air*, Stirling, Scots Independent, nd, p.10.

26 Malcolm Petrie, 'John MacCormick', in James Mitchell and Gerry Hassan (eds.), *Scottish National Party Leaders*, London, Biteback Publishing, p.60.

27 *Hamilton Advertiser*, 26 September 1959.

28 Ibid., 3 October 1959.

29 Official report on the underground fire at Auchengeich colliery, on 18 September 1959, http://www.scottishmining.co.uk/250.html

30 Fifty years later a memorial to the dead miners was unveiled by First Minister Alex Salmond.

31 *Evening Times*, 7 October 1959.

32 *Evening Times*, 9 October 1959.

33 Ian Budge and D.W. Urwin, *Scottish Political Behaviour*, London, Longmans, 1966, p.61.

34 James Mitchell, *Conservatives and the Union*, Edinburgh, Edinburgh University Press, 1990, p.53

35 *Hamilton Advertiser*, 3 March 1967.

36 Ibid.

37 Ibid., 10 March 1967.

38 Ibid.

39 Ibid.

40 Ibid., 23 December 1966.

41 Ibid., 10 March 1967.

42 Roger Davidson and Gayle Davis, *The Sexual State: Sexuality and the Scottish Governance, 1950–80*, Edinburgh, Edinburgh University Press, 2012, p.61.

43 Quoted in Davidson and Davis, 2012, pp.97–126.

44 *Hamilton Advertiser*, 5 May 1967.

45 Ibid., 24 March 1967.

46 Colin McGlashan, 'Nationalists threated Labour's "cradle"', *Observer*, 29 October 1967.

47 Arthur Marwick, *The Sixties: Cultural Revolution in Britain, France, Italy and the United States, c.1958–c.1874*, Oxford, Oxford University Press, 1998, p.37.

48 There are numerous examples of such writing from this time. See, for example, Lucien Pye, *Aspects of Political Development*, Boston, Little Brown, 1966, pp.33–45; Almond, G. and G. Powell, *Comparative Politics: A Developmental Approach*, Boston, Little Brown, 1966, pp.299–332; J. Kautsky, 'An Essay in the Politics of Underdevelopment', in J. Kautsky (ed.), *Political Change in Underdeveloped Societies*, Huntington, Krieger, 1976, pp.25–34). Ethnoregionalism was seen as a residue, moribund political tradition which was anomalous in the modern integrated state, T. Parsons, and N. Smelser, *Economy and Society: A Study in the Integration of Economic and Social Theory*, Glencoe, The Free Press, 1956. Some scholars even suggested that the world was leading 'toward an ultimate integration of societies' even potentially to world government, C.E. Black, *The Dynamics of Modernization: A Study in Comparative History*, New York, Harper & Row, 1966, pp.155, 174. Others argued

that this process was irreversible, Samuel P. Huntington, 'The Change to Change: Modernisation, Development, and Politics', *Comparative Politics*, vol.3, 1971, pp.289–290.

49 In 1962, Welsh nationalist Saunders Lewis had argued for the primacy of the language in a broadcast in which he argued, '...if any kind of self-government for Wales was obtained before Welsh is admitted and used as an official language in local and national administration in the Welsh-speaking areas of our country, then the language will never achieve official status at all, and its death would be quicker than it will be under the rule of England'. Alan Butt Philip, *The Welsh Question 1945–1970*, Cardiff, University of Wales Press, 1975, p.90.

50 *Glasgow Herald*, 7 August 1967; Scots *Independent*, 26 August 1967.

51 Bodleian Library, Oxford, Conservative Party Archive, CPA. CCO 500/50/1, Surveys of Scottish, Welsh and West Country Nationalism, 1967–8. Confidential Paper [by Chris Patten], Nationalism and Regionalism, July 1966.

52 *Scottish Daily Express*, 27 July 1967.

53 Patricia Elton Mayo, *The Roots of Identity: The National Movements in Contemporary European Politics*, London, Allen Lane, 1974, p.1.

54 *Scots Independent*, June 1975.

55 Quoted in Iain McLean, 'The Rise and Fall of the Scottish National Party', *Political Studies*, vol.18, 1970, p.360.

56 *Scottish Daily Express*, 16 June 1962.

57 Keith Webb, *The Growth of Nationalism in Scotland*, Glasgow, The Molendinar Press, 1977, p.101.

58 Ibid., p.103.

59 NLS, Acc.10090/94 Draft Directive for the procedure on the announcement of a by-election, 8 May 1967 from Dr J.C. Lees, Executive Vice Chair Organisation.

60 NLS, Acc.10090/85 Meeting of National Council – 3 September 1966, Report of Executive Vice-Chairman – Organisation, 19 August 1966.

61 Webb, 1977, p.100.

62 Gordon Wilson, *SNP: The Turbulent Years 1960–1990*, Stirling, *Scots Independent*, 2009, p.40.

63 NLS, Acc.10090/94 Letter from Robin Douglas-Home, 53 West Cromwell Road, London, SW5 to Arthur Donaldson, 6 April 1967.

64 NLS, Acc.10090/94 Letter to Robin Douglas-Home, 4 April 1967.

65 'Third party' is used here to refer all parties that challenged the two party dominance rather than a specific third party.

66 David Butler and Anthony King, *The British General Election of 1964*, London, Macmillan and Co. Ltd, 1965, p.356. The SNP averaged 10.7% in seats without a Liberal but only 5.5% where there was a Liberal candidate.

67 James Kellas, 'Scottish Nationalism', in David Butler and Michael Pinto-Duschinsky, *The British General Election of 1970*, Basingstoke, The Macmillan Press, 1971, p.453; Graham Watson, 'Scottish Liberals, Scottish Nationalists and Dreams of a Common Front', *Journal of Liberal Democrat History*, vol.22, 1999, p.6. Grimond was Orkney & Shetland MP 1950–83 and British Liberal leader, 1956–67; Steel became MP in the Scottish Borders 1965–76 and Liberal leader 1976–88; Bannerman was Liberal candidate in the Inverness-shire by-election coming second with 36% of the vote and chaired the Scottish Liberals 1954–64; James Davidson became MP for Aberdeenshire West 1966–70; and Alasdair Mackenzie was Liberal MP for Ross and Cromarty, 1964–70 and was one of Winnie Ewing's sponsors when she took her seat in the Commons.

68 Conservatives (Sir Alec Douglas-Home) 57.4%; Liberals 19.5%; Labour 15.2%; SNP (Arthur Donaldson) 7.3%; Independent Unionist 0.3%; Willie Rushton 0.2%; Light and Dark Blue Conservative Party 0.1%.

69 Douglas was elected to the Commons for Clackmannan and East Stirlingshire in 1970 on his fourth attempt to find a seat, only to lose it to the SNP in 1974 but returned to Parliament in 1979 in Fife. He defected to the SNP in 1990 and stood against Donald Dewar, Labour's Scottish leader, in 1992 but failed to get elected.

70 Paula Somerville, *Through the Maelstrom: A History of the Scottish National Party, 1945–1967*, Stirling, Scots Independent, 2013, p.165.

71 NLS, Acc.10090/81 Reports of National Officer Holders to 33rd annual national conference of SNP, 2–4 June 1967.

72 Ibid., Confidential provisional agenda for the 1967 SNP annual conference, 2–4 June 1967.

73 Ibid., Acc.10090/92 Minutes of NEC, 11 August 1967 with report of Electoral Planning Committee, 21 July 1967.

74 Acc.6038 Scottish National Party Papers, Box 5, Pollok By-Election Report, June 1967.

75 James Kellas, 'Scottish Nationalism' in David Butler and Michael Pinto-Duschinsky, *The British General Election of 1970*, Basingstoke, Macmillan, 1971, p.450.

76 Ibid., p.451.

77 NLS, Acc.6038, Box 5, Pollok By-Election Report, June 1967.

78 David Butler, British General Elections Since 1945, Oxford, Basil Blackwell, 1989, p.97.

79 NLS Acc.6038 Box 5 Pollok By-Election Report, June 1967.

80 Ibid., Acc.10090/80 Report of the Executive Vice-Chairman for Finance Annual National Conference, 2–4 June 1967, Music Hall, 54 George Street, Edinburgh.

81 Ibid., Acc.10090/92 Minutes of Election Planning Committee, 9 June 1967; Acc.10090/94 Draft Directive for the procedure on the announcement of a by-election, 8 May 1967 from Dr J.C. Lees, Executive Vice Chair Organisation.

82 Ibid., Acc.10090/81 Confidential Provisional Agenda for 1967 SNP annual conference 2–4 June 1967.

83 Watson 1999, p.6.

Chapter Two

1 George Downie, *Hamilton Advertiser*'s chief reported in 1967 in 'Ewing rekindles memories of the battlefield dispatch', *The Herald*, 21 September 1999.

2 *Hamilton Advertiser*, 3 November 1967, early edition before result was declared.

3 *Glasgow Herald*, 2 November 1967.

4 *Glasgow Herald*, 2 November 1967; *Evening Times*, 2 November 1967.

5 David Butler and Michael Pinto-Duschinsky, *The British General Election of 1970*, Basingstoke, The Macmillan Press, 1971, p.379.

6 *Daily Record*, 23 October 1967.

7 Reported exclusively in the *Hamilton Advertiser*, 22 September 1967.

8 Roger Smith, 'Stonehouse – An Obituary for a New Town', *Local Government Studies*, vol.4, 1978, pp.57–64.

9 Gordon Wilson, *Pirates of the Air: The Story of Radio Free Scotland*, Stirling, Scots Independent, nd.

10 D.E. Butler and A. King, *The British General Election of 1966*, London, Macmillan, 1966, p.130.

11 D.E. Butler and A. King, *The British General Election of 1966*, London, Macmillan, 1966, pp.130.

12 *Hamilton Advertiser*, 6 May 1966.

13 Ibid., 10 February 1967.

14 Ibid., 17 March 1967.

15 Ibid., 17 March 1967.

16 Ibid., 12 May 1967.
17 Ibid., 12 May 1967.
18 *Glasgow Herald*, 26 September 1967.
19 Ibid., 25 October 1967.
20 Ibid., 24 October 1967.
21 Richard Crossman, *The Diaries of a Cabinet Minister*, vol.2, London, Hamish Hamilton, 1966, p.581.
22 *Hamilton Advertiser*, 7 April 1967.
23 *The Times*, 3 March 1967.
24 *Hansard*, Commons, 5 July 1967, vol.749, col.1843.
25 *Hansard*, Commons, 5 July 1967, col.1852.
26 *Daily Record*, 7 July 1967.
27 *Glasgow Herald*, Tuesday, August 29, 1967.
28 *Daily Record*, 20 October 1967.
29 *Scottish Daily Express*, 25 August 1967.
30 Max Nicholson, *The System: the misgovernment of Britain*, New York, McGraw-Hill Book Company, 1967.
31 William Waldegrave, *A Different Kind of Weather: A Memoir*, London, Constable, 2015, Kindle version location 726. Waldegrave recounts that Nicholson turned down a knighthood offered by the Thatcher Government.
32 Richard Crossman, *The Diaries of a Cabinet Minister*, vol.2, London, Hamish Hamilton, 1966, pp.492, 494.
33 MacDiarmid's politics have been the source of much ill-informed commentary. The most reasoned and properly researched work is Bob Purdie, *Hugh MacDiarmid: Black, Green, Red and Tartan*, Cardiff, Welsh Academic Press, 2012.
34 Michael Grieve had a column 'The Voice of Scotland' in the *Record* in which he offered nationalist views and wrote scathing critiques of Labour. He became SNP Vice Chair for Publicity, 1969–72 and stood for Parliament in 1970 and 1979.
35 *Daily Record*, Tuesday, September 26, 1967.
36 Ibid.
37 NLS, Acc.10090/94 Confidential note from Russell Thomson to Douglas Drysdale, 11 April 1966.
38 Ibid.
39 NLS, Acc.10090/94 Letter to Dr Robert McIntyre from Gordon Wilson, 2 August 1966.

40 Ibid., Chairman's report, Meeting of National Council, 3 September 1966, 24 August 1966.

41 Ibid., Meeting of National Executive, 12 August 1966. Report of Vice Chairman Organisation.

42 At that time, candidates had to be designated as prospective to avoid incurring any campaign expenditure being included in permissible limits at an election. Someone described as a party's candidate in the weeks, months and years before an election would have to declare such expenditure.

43 *Scots Independent*, 17 September 1966.

44 At his death in 1999 at age 87, Braid was Scotland's longest serving councillor having first been elected in Fife 55 years before and having served on a number of occasions as Provost, though as an Independent. One of the most frequently told stories about him, and recounted by John Lloyd in the *Financial Times* was of the occasion when he backed his car into St Monans harbour after a few drinks escaping unharmed. John Lloyd, 'Mixed memories of a Scottish childhood', *Financial Times*, 12 September 2014.

45 NLS, Acc.6038, SNP papers, Minutes of Meeting of the Organisation Committee Held in 16 North St Andrew Street, Edinburgh on Saturday, 13 August 1966.

46 Gordon Wilson, *SNP: The Turbulent Years. 1960–1990*. Stirling, Scots Independent Ltd., 2009, p.37.

47 Winnie Ewing, *Stop the World: The Autobiography of Winnie Ewing*, Edinburgh, Birlinn Limited, 2004, p.3.

48 Hugh Macdonald, John McAteer Obituary, *Scots Independent*, April 1977. Quoted in Ewen Angus Cameron, 'Arthur Donaldson', in James Mitchell and Gerry Hassan (eds.), *Scottish National Party Leaders*, London, Biteback Publishing, 2016, p.235.

49 Macdonald stood in Clackmannan and East Stirlingshire in 1970, coming third with 15.5 per cent of the vote – 5 per cent down on the 1966 election due to the intervention of a Liberal candidate. In 1974, Macdonald stood in Hamilton in both elections in 1974, coming within 3,333 votes of taking the seat from Labour.

50 NLS, Acc.10090/112 Letter from Winifred Ewing to Dr McIntyre, 6 September 1966.

51 Hugh MacDonald, 'John McAteer', *Scots Independent*, April 1977.

52 Interview with Kate McAteer.

53 NLS Acc.6308. Correspondence of and to Arthur Donaldson and meetings.

54 Tam Dalyell, *The Question of Scotland: Devolution and After*, Edinburgh, Birlinn 2016.
55 Ibid., p.24.
56 James Halliday, *Yours for Scotland*, Stirling, Scots Independent, 2011, p.20.
57 This would likely have been at a presentation to Gibson at the Royal Stuart Hotel, Glasgow, 18 February 1966.
58 *Hamilton Advertiser*, 10 November 1967.
59 Ibid., 15 September 1967.
60 *Sunday Post*, 5 November 1967.
61 NLS, Acc. 10090/112 Letter from Winifred Ewing to Dr McIntyre, 6 September 1966.
62 NLS, Acc.6038, Minutes of National Council meeting, 17 June 1967.
63 *Daily Record*, 20 September 1967.
64 *Hamilton Advertiser*, 14 July 1967.
65 Ibid.
66 As Lord Wilson of Langside, he would become chair of *Scotland Says No*, the anti-devolution campaign organisation in the 1979 devolution referendum and publicly supported the Conservatives in the subsequent general election.
67 *Hamilton Advertiser*, 1 September 1967.
68 *Daily Record*, 4 November 1967.
69 *Hamilton Advertiser*, 1 September 1967.
70 Mark Stuart, *John Smith: A Life*, London, Politico, 2005, p.61.
71 Information from David Rollo.
72 *Daily Record*, 23 October 1967.
73 Tam Dalyell, *The Question of Scotland – Devolution and After*, Edinburgh, Birlinn Limited, 2016, p.22.
74 There was already an MP from the village. John Ryan was elected as a 26-year-old Labour Member for Uxbridge, Middlesex.
75 *The Herald*, 21 September 1999.
76 *Hamilton Advertiser*, 22 September 1967.
77 Ibid.
78 H.J. Hanham, *Scottish Nationalism*, London, Faber and Faber, 1969, pp.185–186.
79 *Daily Record*, 23 October 1967.
80 Ibid.

81 The study involved two blocks of flats in Dundee which were similar socio-demographically. Working with the local Labour Party, the academics found that there was a ten per cent difference in turnout in the block which was the subject of intense canvassing and leafleting compared with the other which received no campaigning. As this was a solid Labour area, there was no activity from opponents. John Bochel and David Denver, 'The impact of the campaign on the results of local government elections', *British Journal of Political Science*, vol.2, 1972, 239–243.

82 For a good summary of current thinking see Paul Whiteley, 'Do campaigns make a difference?', *Oxford Research Encyclopedia of Politics*.

83 *Scots Independent*, 14 October 1967.

84 NLS, Acc.10090/92 Minutes of meeting of NEC, 18 August 1967.

85 NLS, Acc.6038, Box 5, SNP Newsletter, August 1967.

86 *Scots Independent*, 9 September 1967.

87 Ibid., 2 September 1967.

88 Ibid., 9 September 1967.

89 *Observer*, 29 October 1967.

90 Ibid.

91 *Hamilton Advertiser*, 20 October 1967.

92 *Evening Times*, 18 October 1967; *Hamilton Advertiser*, 20 October 1967.

93 *The Herald*, 21 September 1999.

94 *Hamilton Advertiser*, 27 October 1967.

95 National Archives, Kew, T328/227. Letter from Gregor Mackenzie MP to Harold [Lever] dated 11/10/6.

96 Ibid. Draft letter to Gregor Mackenzie MP from Treasury.

97 Smillie, from Larkhall, was son of the miners' leader who played a key role in transferring miners' support from the Liberal Party to Labour, helped establish the Scottish Trades Union Congress, was a founding member of the Scottish Labour Party, with Keir Hardie, and the Independent Labour Party.

98 *Sunday Mail*, 29 October 1967.

99 Ibid.

100 *Daily Record*, 31 October 1967. The poll involved a team of *Record* journalists asking a 'careful' sample of 440 people how they would vote.

101 *Hamilton Advertiser*, 27 October 1967.

102 Ibid.

103 *Glasgow Herald*, 2 November 1967.

104 *Daily Record*, 28 October 1967.

105 *Observer*, 29 October 1967.
106 *Hamilton Advertiser*, 6 October 1967.
107 Ibid., 27 October 1967.
108 Ibid., 25 August 1967.
109 *Hamilton Advertiser*, 2 September 1966.
110 SET was replaced with Value Added Tax in 1973.
111 *Observer*, 29 October 1967.
112 Richard Crossman, *The Diaries of a Cabinet Minister*, vol.2, London, Hamish Hamilton, 1966, p.530.
113 *Glasgow Herald*, 5 October 1967.
114 *The Times*, 31 October 1967.
115 *Hamilton Advertiser*, 17 March 1967.
116 Ibid., 15 September 1967.
117 *Glasgow Herald*, 22 August 1966.
118 *Scots Independent*, 1 July 1967.
119 *Glasgow Herald*, 10 October 1967.
120 *Observer*, 5 November 1967.
121 *Hamilton Advertiser*, 8 September 1967.
122 Ibid., 8 September 1967.
123 *Scottish Daily Express*, 23 September 1967.
124 Bodleian Library, Oxford, Conservative Party Archive, CPA. CCO 500/50/1, Surveys of Scottish, Welsh and West Country Nationalism, 1967–68. Tommy Thompson, Conservative and Unionist Central Office to Chairman, 28 September 1967.
125 *Glasgow Herald*, 4 October 1967.
126 Bodleian Library, Oxford, Conservative Party Archive, CPA. CCO 500/50/1, Surveys of Scottish, Welsh and West Country Nationalism, 1967–68. Opinion Research Centre: A Survey on Hamilton Constituency, carried out for Conservative Central Office.
127 *Scotsman*, 30 October 1967.
128 Ibid.
129 D.E. Butler and A. King, The British General Election of 1966, London, Macmillan, 1966, pp.104–105.
130 NLS Acc.6038 Box 5 Letter from Winifred Ewing to Arthur Donaldson, 11 September 1967.
131 *Evening Times*, 31 October 1967.
132 Daily Record, 3 November 1967.

133 One estimate suggests that MacGillveray's Alba Pools raised over £200,000 in five years. Keith Webb, *The Growth of Nationalism in Scotland*, Glasgow, The Molendinar Press, 1977, p.101.

134 *Hamilton Advertiser*, 27 October 1967.

135 Winnie Ewing, *Stop the World: The Autobiography of Winnie Ewing*, Edinburgh, Birlinn Limited, 2004, pp.12–13.

136 *Hamilton Advertiser*, 3 November 1967.

137 Ibid.

138 Ibid.

139 George Downie, 'Ewing rekindles memories of the battlefield dispatch', *The Herald*, 21 September 1999.

140 *Hamilton Advertiser*, 10 November 1967.

141 Ibid., 3 November 1967.

Chapter Three

1 James Kellas, 'Scottish Nationalism' in David Butler and Michael Pinto-Duschinsky, The British General Election of 1970, London, Macmillan, 1971, p.446.

2 Scots Independent, front page editorial, 11 November 1967.

3 Iain Ogilvie, 'Why Labour Crashed at Hamilton, New Statesman, 10 November 1967.

4 National Archives, Note from Treasury official to colleagues, T328/227, 14 November 1967,

5 Cairncross, Alec, *The Wilson Years: a Treasury, 1964–69*, London, Historian's Press, 1997, p.243.

6 *Evening Citizen*, 21 November 1967.

7 Jack Brand, *The National Movement in Scotland*, London, Routledge & Kegan Paul, 1978, p.132–33.

8 *The Times*, 31 October 1967.

9 Winnie Ewing, *Stop the World: The Autobiography of Winnie Ewing*, Edinburgh, Birlinn Limited, 2004, p.5.

10 *Scotsman*, 29 October 1967.

11 Kellas, 'Scottish Nationalism', in David Butler and Michael Pinto-Duschinsky, *The British General Election of 1970*, Basingstoke, The Macmillan Press, 1971, p.452.

12 *Scottish Daily Express*, 5 December 1967.

13 Harry Reid, *Deadline: The Story of the Scottish Press*, Edinburgh, St Andrew Press, 2006, p.9.

14 'How Scotland Should Be Governed', *The Scotsman*, Edinburgh. Also *The Scotsman*, 3,5,6,7 February 1968.

15 Letter from Gordon Wilson, 23 December 1967. I am grateful to Ewen Cameron for this information.

16 NLS Acc.6038. British Broadcasting Corporation Week 48 An Audience Research Report Confidential Party political broadcast on behalf of the Scottish Nationalist [sic] Party by Mrs Winifred Ewing MP Thursday, 30 November 1967, 6.55–7.00pm Radio 4 (Scotland) Audience Research Department, BBC, 17 January 1968.

17 NLS Acc.6038, Minutes of meeting of SNP NEC, 12 January 1968.

18 *Evening Times*, 7 November 1967.

19 *Scottish Daily Express*, 25 November 1967.

20 *Glasgow Herald*, 18 December 1967.

21 *Scottish Daily Express*, 17 November 1967.

22 National Archives, Note from Treasury official to colleagues, T328/227, 14 November 1967,

23 *Hamilton Advertiser*, 10 November 2011.

24 Rhys Evans, *Gwynfor Evans: A Portrait of a Patriot*, Talybont, Ceredigion, Y Lolfa Cf., 2008, p.285.

25 *Hansard*, Commons, 20 November 1967, vol.754, cols.977–980.

26 Report of the Committee on the Age of Majority (Latey), HMSO, London, Command Paper No. 3342, 1967.

27 Ibid., para.34.

28 *Hansard*, Commons, 20 November 1967, vol.754, col. 978.

29 *Scottish Daily Express*, 18 November 1967.

30 *Hansard*, Commons, 20 November 1967, vol.754, col. 980.

31 *The Scotsman*, 23 May 1968.

32 *Hansard*, Commons, 24 May 1968, vol. 765, col.1103.

33 NLS, Acc.6018, Letter from R.I. Webster, Pretoria, Republic of South Africa, 16 December 1967.

34 Randall Hansen, 'The Kenyan Asians, British Politics, and the Commonwealth Immigrants Act, 1968', The Historical Journal, vol.42, p.810.

35 Maurice Miller, Emrys Hughes, John P. Mackintosh.

36 *Hamilton Advertiser*, 3 November 1967.

37 Ibid., 3 November 1967.

38 Ibid., 10 November 1967.

39 Ibid.

40 *Glasgow Herald*, 5 November 1967.
41 *Scottish Daily Express*, 9 November 1967; *Evening Times*, 8 November 1967.
42 *Hamilton Advertiser*, 10 November 1967.
43 Kellas, 'Scottish Nationalism', in David Butler and Michael Pinto-Duschinsky, The British General Election of 1970, Basingstoke, The Macmillan Press, 1971, p.452.
44 *Glasgow Herald*, 4 November 1967.
45 *Glasgow Herald* editorial, 4 November 1967.
46 *Evening Times*, 7 November 1967.
47 *Daily Record*, 9 November 1967.
48 Ibid.
49 Richard Crossman, *The Diaries of a Cabinet Minister*, vol.2, London, Hamish Hamilton, 1966, p.550.
50 Tam Dalyell, *The Question of Scotland – Devolution and After*, Edinburgh, Birlinn Limited, 2016, p.22.
51 *Glasgow Herald*, 25 October 1967.
52 Iain Ogilvie, 'Why Labour Crashed at Hamilton, New Statesman, 10 November 1967.
53 James Mitchell, *Governing Scotland: The Invention of Administrative Devolution*, Basingstoke, MacMillan, 2003.
54 *Glasgow Herald*, 5 November 1967.
55 Daniel Awdry, MP for Chippenham, *Hansard*, Commons, 20 December 1967, vol.756, col.1375.
56 *Glasgow Herald*, 11 December 1967.
57 *Hansard*, Commons, vol.753, 1 November 1967, col.307.
58 NLS, Acc.9588, George Lawson Papers, Scottish Labour Group Executive Committee Report for submission to Group meeting 5 March 1968.
59 Hansard, Commons, 13 March 1967, vol.743, col.39; 24 April 1967, vol.745, col.205W.
60 Ibid., 14 November 1967, vol.754, col.262.
61 NLS, Acc.9588, George Lawson Papers, Letter to Dick Buchanan MP from William Marshall, Scottish Secretary of the Labour Party Scottish Council, 20 November 1968.
62 Ibid., 12 October 1967.
63 *Glasgow Herald*, 25 November 1967.
64 James Mitchell, *Devolution in the United Kingdom*, Manchester, Manchester University Press, 2009, pp.57–58.

65 *The Herald*, 21 September 1999.

66 Bodleian Library, Oxford, Conservative Party Archive, CPA. CCO 500/50/1, Surveys of Scottish, Welsh and West Country Nationalism, 1967–68. Opinion Research Centre: A Survey on Hamilton Constituency, carried out for Conservative Central Office.

67 *Glasgow Herald*, 27 November 1967.

68 Ibid., 25 November 1967.

69 Bodleian Library, Oxford, Conservative Party Archive, CPA. CCO 500/50/1, Surveys of Scottish, Welsh and West Country Nationalism, 1967–8. Memo, Tommy Thompson to The Chairman, 27 Mar 1968.

70 Bodleian Library, Oxford, Conservative Party Archive, CPA. CCO 500/50/1, Surveys of Scottish, Welsh and West Country Nationalism, 1967–68. Tommy Thompson to Sir Gilmour Menzies Anderson, 27 March 1968.

71 'A Better Tomorrow', Conservative Party manifesto 1970, http://www.conservativemanifesto.com/1970/1970-conservative-manifesto.shtml

72 *Glasgow Herald*, 20 March 1970.

73 Ibid., 5 November 1967.

74 Hansard, House of Lords, 6 December 1967, vol. 287, col.705.

75 *Evening Times*, 8 November 1967.

76 *The Scotsman*, 1 July 967.

77 *Glasgow Herald*, 31 October 1969.

78 Ibid.

79 Ibid.

80 Michael McManus, *Jo Grimond: Towards the Sound of Gunfire*, Edinburgh, Birlinn, 2001, p.308.

81 *Glasgow Herald*, 21 March 1970.

82 Alex Eadie and Jim Sillars, *Don't Butcher Scotland's Future*, Published by Eadie and Sillars, 1968.

83 H.M. Drucker, *Breakaway: The Scottish Labour Party*, Edinburgh, EUSPB, nd. p.14.

84 *Glasgow Herald*, 20 March 1970.

85 Ibid., 23 March 1970.

86 Ibid., 23 March 1970.

87 David Butler and Michael Pinto-Duschinsky, *The British General Election of 1970*, Basingstoke, The Macmillan Press, 1971, p.403.

88 James Mitchell, *Devolution in the United Kingdom*, Manchester, Manchester University Press, 2009, p.113.

Conclusion

1 Arthur Marwick, *The Sixties: Cultural Revolution in Britain, France, Italy and the United States, c.1958–c.1974*, Oxford, Oxford University Press, 1998, p.3.

2 The source of this quote is disputed though a number of sources have been suggested. According to Stephen Goranson it originally appeared in the *Los Angelos Times*, 13 June 1982. http://quoteinvestigator.com/2010/05/07/remember-1960s/

3 James G. Kellas, 'Scottish Nationalism', in David Butler and Michael Pinto-Duschinsky, *The British General Election of 1970*, Basingstoke, Macmillan, 1971, pp.451–452.

4 Tam Dalyell, *The Question of Scotland – Devolution and After*, Edinburgh, Birlinn Limited, 2016, p.20.

5 Pippa Norris, *British By-Elections: The Volatile Electorate*, Oxford, Clarendon Press, 1990, p.1.

6 Ibid., p.224.

7 R.E. Dundas, 'The SNP after Hamilton', *Glasgow Herald*, 10 November 1967.

8 Norris 1990, pp.224–225.

9 Arnold Kemp, *The Hollow Drum: Scotland Since the War*, Edinburgh, Mainstream, 1993, p.96.

10 *Hansard*, Commons, 10 November 1967, vol.753, col.194w.

11 Interviews with author at various times.

12 Iain McLean, 'The Politics of Nationalism and Devolution', Political Studies, vol. 25, 1977, p.427; and 'Devolution', Political Quarterly, vol.47, 1976; Harry Lazer, 'Devolution, Ethnic Nationalism, and Populism in the United Kingdom', Publius, vol.7, 1977.

13 Hank Johnston, *What Is A Social Movement?*, Cambridge, Polity Press, 2014, p.37.

14 Anthony Oberschall, *Conflict and Social Movements*, Englewood Cliffs, N.J., Prentice-Hall, 1973.

15 W.G. Runciman, *Relative Deprivation and Social Justice*, London, Routledge and Kegan Paul, 1966.

16 Gavin McCrone, *Scotland's Future: The Economics of Nationalism*, Oxford, Basil Blackwell, 1969, p.11.

17 Schwarz, J.E., 'The Scottish National Party: Non-violent Separatism and Theories of Violence', in I.K. Feierabend, R.L. Feierabend and R.R. Gurr (eds), Anger, Violence and Politics: Theories and Research, Prentice-Hall, 1972.

18 Brooks, Roger Alan, *Scottish Nationalism: Relative Deprivation and Social Mobility*, Unpublished Michigan State University PhD, 1973.

19 Keith Webb and Eric Hall, 'Explanations of the rise of political nationalism in Scotland', Glasgow, University of Strathclyde, Studies in Public Policy No.15, 1978, p.14.

20 Rokkan, Stein and Urwin, Derek, (1983), *Economy Territory Identity*, London, Sage, 1983, p.139.

21 *Glasgow Herald*, March 11, 1970.

22 George Downie, 'Ewing rekindles memories of the battlefield dispatch', *The Herald*, 21 September 1999.

23 Ibid.

24 Jimmi Østergaard Nielsen and Stuart Ward, '"Cramped and Restricted at Home?" Scottish Separatism at Empire's End', Transactions of the Royal Historical Society, vol.25, 2015, pp.159–185.

25 Ibid., p.171.

26 Ibid., p.181; Stuart Ward, 'The "New Nationalism" in Australia, Canada and New Zealand: Civic Culture in the Wake of the British World', in Kate Darian-Smith, Stuart MacIntyre and Patricia Grimshaw (eds.), Britishness Abroad: Transnational Movements and Imperial Cultures, Melbourne, Melbourne University Press, 2007, pp.231–63.

27 The notion of relative political deprivation draws on work by Walker Connor who was critical of economic explanations of nationalism and proposed the alternative notion of relative political deprivation. See Walker Connor, 'From a Theory of Relative Economic Deprivation Towards a Theory of Relative Political Deprivation', in M. Keating and J. McGarry, Minority Nationalism and the Changing International Order, Oxford, Oxford University Press, 2003.

28 Report of the Royal Commission on Scottish Affairs (Balfour), Edinburgh, HMSO, 1954, p.12, para.14.

29 *Scottish Daily Express*, 11 November 1967.

30 James Kellas, *The Scottish Political System*, Cambridge, Cambridge University Press, 1973.

Luath Press Limited

committed to publishing well written books worth reading

LUATH PRESS takes its name from Robert Burns, whose little collie Luath (*Gael.*, swift or nimble) tripped up Jean Armour at a wedding and gave him the chance to speak to the woman who was to be his wife and the abiding love of his life. Burns called one of 'The Twa Dogs' Luath after Cuchullin's hunting dog in Ossian's *Fingal*. Luath Press was established in 1981 in the heart of Burns country, and now resides a few steps up the road from Burns' first lodgings on Edinburgh's Royal Mile.

Luath offers you distinctive writing with a hint of unexpected pleasures.

ILLUSTRATION: IAN KELLAS

Most bookshops in the UK, the US, Canada, Australia, New Zealand and parts of Europe either carry our books in stock or can order them for you. To order direct from us, please send a £sterling cheque, postal order, international money order or your credit card details (number, address of cardholder and expiry date) to us at the address below. Please add post and packing as follows: UK – £1.00 per delivery address; overseas surface mail – £2.50 per delivery address; overseas airmail – £3.50 for the first book to each delivery address, plus £1.00 for each additional book by airmail to the same address. If your order is a gift, we will happily enclose your card or message at no extra charge.

Luath Press Limited
543/2 Castlehill
The Royal Mile
Edinburgh EH1 2ND
Scotland

Telephone: 0131 225 4326 (24 hours)
email: sales@luath.co.uk
Website: www.luath.co.uk